DEATH

Told through the lens of her own experiences, Lois West Bristow's ability to weave together emotion with the intellectual study of death makes for a thought provoking read. It gave me pause to consider death in a different way, but doing so brought both understanding and peace.
Chery Popiel, Retired Teacher

• • • • •

Dr. Bristow is a worthy wordsmith, gifted in her choice and flow of words. Elegant and direct. As soon as I read the stunning poem, I knew this book was right for me. And then came the commanding first sentence in the introduction. "I knew that I wanted to be present at my death." I've always imagined my ideal death to be simply falling asleep never to awaken.

I felt so close to the author. She and I share common ground—the quest for the sacred, consciousness, meaning, healing, soul. Perhaps because I feel she is so vigilantly truthful in all she shares? The telling of Charles' dying astounded and held me.

I was struck by Jung's quote, "I am and remain in search of myself, of the truth peculiar to myself." "Now I am." "It is—not was or will be." "Being present." All a major turning point for me, unfolding welcomed new perspectives and experiences. The vast and steadfast awareness I experience in meditation or any quiet moment of within seems to be compatible with the author's concept of "keel of contentment," the "being ourselves," of knowing our "who-we-are-ness."

When I first read the words "the sacredness of death" I was surprised that I was surprised. Yes, death is sacred, too sacred to miss. I want to be conscious at my death. Being aware makes a difference, even works wonders. Not until reading

this book had I truly pondered dying with awareness. This book is timely. It fulfills the promises others have written about it. It's a gift of truths and inspiration for weaving our ways through life and death. It's a gem.
Jeralyn Scott McCarthy
County Cork, Ireland

• • • • •

An interesting and thought-provoking book. I am impressed by the author's ability to take a difficult subject and make it accessible. The book is beautifully and gives the reader insight into the end-of-life experience. Kudos for author Dr. Lois West Bristow.
Louise Stewart, MD

• • • • •

I appreciate the wisdom shared in the book, *Death Comes Not as a Stranger*. At 27, I may not have a deep grasp of my own impending death, but I do, like most, struggle with the fears and worries that follow the unrealistic expectation of staying young, thin, and happy. To hear someone speak of unhappiness being O.K. releases us from questioning what is *wrong* with us, it lets us accept ourselves and get back to moving more deeply through our experiences. The author's sharing of personal stories and inner journeys illustrates the examination of these fears and of death and allows the reader to pick up deeply important gems along the way.
Julie Benda, Artist and Gardener

• • • • •

What I liked about your book, which was lent to me by a friend, was the relief I felt when you reached 'the end' without plugging any partisan belief system, while recognizing that

the life of spirit was beginning. I haven't got a copy of your book under my nose to check your words, but I will have one soon. I have always thought like you think, that Death must be the second most amazing experience of our lives. Your book helps me to welcome Death as an ally with a growing sense of exploration and thoughtfulness.
Naomi Brandel, London

• • • • •

Dear Dr. Lois W. Bristow:

I read your book *Death Comes Not as a Stranger* and found it answers many questions for me. I have lived some eighty odd years and seen death up close in the Pacific during World War II. In 1971, I sustained a gunshot wound to the chest during a robbery. The first doctor that saw me said "Get him out of here. I don't want him dying on me. Take him to General Hospital in LA." There I was told had the wound been just an inch to the left, my heart would have been gone. For three days I was on the critical list. In 1991 I had prostate cancer of a severe nature. An operation has allowed me to live twenty-two more years.

Each time I saw or faced death I thought of the hereafter and all the different stages of life I have lived. It was difficult to deal with the events and stages of life until I read your book. Many thanks.
Dr. Henry G. Clute, DVM

• • • • •

"I loved this book. I'm in my eighties and it reminded me to appreciate every day."
Barbara Thomson, Retired

• • • • •

Although recommended by two people I admire, my initial thought was "This book is not for me!" After all, I'm a healthy forty-six-year old who is already comfortable with the idea of death. I erroneously thought this book was written for those who are terminally ill or their loved ones or perhaps practitioners who regularly encounter death. But as I began reading, it felt as though this book had been written specifically for me. It reminded me that death is not just something that happens to others, but is something that will happen to me.

I hope to grow wise for many years to come. It matters not the count of candles on my last birthday cake, there *will be* a last cake. This book reminds me to savor every bite, because with or without a doctor-diagnosed death sentence, we are all dying. As I embrace the idea of my own death, I live a more authentic life. Death, when it does come for me, will not come as a stranger but as an old and trusted friend. In the meantime death waits and inspires.

Kimberly Davis, Business Owner

• • • • •

With insights of depth psychology and through story masterfully told, one is carried along a path, sometimes humorous, always perceptive, allowing one to reflect on making peace with death. More than just a part of life, death in all its forms is explored a way to wholeness. Read this book written by a wise, educated, and courageous crone guiding others as she is guided by the wildness championed in her heart and embrace your own journey of really living.

Jacqueline Leeba, PhD Candidate Depth Psychology

• • • • •

Death Comes Not as a Stranger brings refreshing insights gained through an array of various perspectives and thoughtful study, offering new and intriguing ways of looking at the meaning of life as well as death. Don't miss this book. Anyone facing death (and that is everyone) should read it! It will give you the confidence and wisdom to embrace your own death as the ultimate life experience, to find meaning in the loss of those close to you, and expand your understanding of life itself.

Joy Ibsen
Editor of Church and Life

• • • • •

As a recent survivor of a ruptured brain aneurysm, an experience that caused me to look both life and death squarely in the eye, I especially appreciate this book. Lois West Bristow has written an honest, graceful book about how she came to confront the inevitability of death and, in so doing, was freed to live the full life she is living. By offering her own experiences, bathed in reflection and the wisdom of age, she prompts readers to do the same, to embrace the fullness of life as we make peace with death's inevitability. Along the way, she raises critical questions that surround death in modern America. Dr. Bristow writes in a clear, engaging style and has produced an insightful book on a topic that affects us all.

Janet Jensen, Minnesota

• • • • •

This book made me laugh at myself when I saw how much time, money, and effort I've wasted getting caught up in pretending that I could stay young. I'm 52, take care of myself, am healthy, and have a fulfilling life. When I realized I look fine being 52, I felt better about myself than I've ever felt. This book isn't just about death. It's also about life.

Dr. Richard Nagy, DDS

• • • • •

Although her work demonstrates rigor and academic discipline, Dr. Bristow's words do not lose their poetic grace as she uses story to bring theory alive and into the common experience of ordinary lives.

Malca Lebell, PhD, LCSW

• • • • •

With her refined and poetic use of language, Dr. Lois West Bristow approaches the often-difficult subject of death with grace and intelligence, shining a new light into what may be the greatest mystery of all, the natural transformation of death.

Shemai Rodriquez, Writer

• • • • •

This profoundly tender dialogue deserves appreciation and reflection. Dr. Lois West Bristow brings the aging process into consciousness while honoring the experiences of loss and concerns we have for our own mortality. It holds meaning for individuals, families, and communities as they navigate the thresholds of life held within the shadows of death.

Martha Feng, LMFT, PhD(c)

Death Comes Not as a Stranger:

Befriending Death & Finding Peace

Lois West Bristow PhD

BALBOA
PRESS
A DIVISION OF HAY HOUSE

Copyright © 2014 Lois West Bristow PhD.

Cover Art: Greg Higgins: Author Photo; Dottie Rickolson: Cover Design: Judith Baerg

All rights reserved. No part of this book may be used or reproduced by any means, graphic, electronic, or mechanical, including photocopying, recording, taping or by any information storage retrieval system without the written permission of the publisher except in the case of brief quotations embodied in critical articles and reviews.

Balboa Press books may be ordered through booksellers or by contacting:

Balboa Press
A Division of Hay House
1663 Liberty Drive
Bloomington, IN 47403
www.balboapress.com
1 (877) 407-4847

Because of the dynamic nature of the Internet, any web addresses or links contained in this book may have changed since publication and may no longer be valid. The views expressed in this work are solely those of the author and do not necessarily reflect the views of the publisher, and the publisher hereby disclaims any responsibility for them.

The author of this book does not dispense medical advice or prescribe the use of any technique as a form of treatment for physical, emotional, or medical problems without the advice of a physician, either directly or indirectly. The intent of the author is only to offer information of a general nature to help you in your quest for emotional and spiritual well-being. In the event you use any of the information in this book for yourself, which is your constitutional right, the author and the publisher assume no responsibility for your actions.

Any people depicted in stock imagery provided by Thinkstock are models, and such images are being used for illustrative purposes only. Certain stock imagery © Thinkstock.

Printed in the United States of America.

ISBN: 978-1-4525-1838-1 (sc)
ISBN: 978-1-4525-1840-4 (hc)
ISBN: 978-1-4525-1839-8 (e)

Library of Congress Control Number: 2014912460

Balboa Press rev. date: 8/15/2014

DEDICATION

To my son Derek Ellis,
my daughter Sheridyn McClain,
my grandsons
Trevor, Trent, and Slater Ellis,
my granddaughters
Ashley Kristyn Ellis and Kaitlyn McClain
and
my great-granddaughter
Dakota Kathleen Ellis
and
in memory of
my son Brad Ellis
(1953-2003)

AUTHOR'S COMMENT

Work on my dissertation planted the seeds and served as one of many resources for writing this book. Stories come from the experiences of others as well as from my own. On occasion and where appropriate, the names of people involved and the settings in which the incidents took place have been changed. The emotional essence of each story remains true to each original experience. Please visit me at:

www.loiswestbristow.com.

ACKNOWLEDGMENTS

Rarely does one write a book alone. Without those who have the courage to be forthright, the good sense to recognize where things do not hold together, and the ability to find errors, this book would not have come into being. My love and gratitude far exceed the capacity of these words to express my appreciation.

Diane Huerta, you are a treasured friend with an exceptional eye. Delores Buettgenbach, your moving stories inspire and comfort us. Shemai Rodriguez, the windows you open to rich customs of other cultures are invaluable. Karin Eide, once again I benefit from your keen eye. Linda Pelka, your courage and clarity are invaluable. Mark Kelly, your ability to come up with crucial information at precisely the right time amazes me. Dottie Richolson, a special thank you. You help has been invaluable. Judy Baerg, your dedication to quality garners respect and love. Greg Higgins, your art lifts the soul.

CONTENTS

DANCING 1

INTRODUCTION
    Wanting To Know 3

CHAPTER ONE
    The Bookends: Birth and Death 9

CHAPTER TWO
    Turning Points 19

CHAPTER THREE
    The Eternal Now: The Space Between 27

CHAPTER FOUR
    Aging Gracefully Western Style 35

CHAPTER FIVE
    Alienation from the Natural 47

CHAPTER SIX
    Flirting with Death: Practice Runs 59

CHAPTER SEVEN
    Being with Death 69

CHAPTER EIGHT
    The Ultimate Loss 77

CHAPTER NINE
    The Purpose of Pain 87

CHAPTER TEN
Hospice and Palliative Care 97

CHAPTER ELEVEN
Charles and Alicia 105

CHAPTER TWELVE
Rites, Rituals, and Ceremonies 113

CHAPTER THIRTEEN
Searching for the Sacred 121

CHAPTER FOURTEEN
Falling and Getting Back Up 129

CHAPTER FIFTEEN
Dying: A New Paradigm 137

CHAPTER SIXTEEN
Walking Each Day with Death 145

CHAPTER SEVENTEEN
The Last Dance 153

APPENDIX 157

RECOMMENDED READING 171

ABOUT THE AUTHOR 173

ENDNOTES 175

DANCING

Unbeknownst to me
the dance I dance so fluidly
is led by an unseen partner,
while all along I thought I danced alone
in stunning grace.
Willingly held in the arms of my shadows,
I am swirled away
to dance with grand precision
the repetitious steps over and again.
Treacherous
are the steps I thought sublime.
Cautiously, new steps take form,
this time danced alone until
the music stops abruptly.
This dance is over.
Yet all the while I have known
the last dance waits for everyone, for me.
When Death extends its hand in invitation,
may I take it willingly and with grace,
yielding into waiting arms
and onto the sacred dance floor
of the vaguely familiar yet strangely unknown.
Will I keep alive
the sparks of wonder and of mystery?

INTRODUCTION
WANTING TO KNOW

Years ago I knew that I wanted to be present at my death; I wanted to know what would happen. Although aware that death was a huge event, my curiosity at the time was somewhat superficial. Over time that superficiality gave way to a profound and tenacious need to know. Incidents occurred that brought the reality of death to the forefront, where it demanded that it be addressed. Slowly and steadily pieces fell together, and new perspectives about death came forth. This book is the story of that drawn-out, irregular, and on-going interaction with death, first as a concept, then as a reality, and finally as an eerily comforting presence.

Initially, addressing death took place from a distance. It was something sad that happened to someone else that primarily impacted the family and close friends of the deceased. While others experienced sadness and sympathy, their lives were not deeply affected. When people close to me died, death became real, unfriendly, and fear-laden. Mourning was a mix of sadness, loss, and the fear of death itself. Those first glimpses were followed by experiences that opened doors to deeper understandings of the far-reaching and all-embracing dread of death that is present in so many of us. With time, bits of understanding coalesced, and my feelings and views about death shifted. As one aspect of death was resolved, another arose. A long road lay ahead before I would find peace with my own death.

It was easy to ignore the finiteness of life, even though I was aware that acknowledging life's temporality heightened a person's appreciation of life. Evidence of life's beginning through birth and ending through death surrounds us. Our embracing both entry and exit holds the potential of giving life urgency and focus, yet our fears stay with us. The sixteenth-century French social philosopher, Michael Montaigne, an astute critic with the ear of a skeptic, wisely reminds us that "Death is part of the order of the Universe, 'tis a part of the life of the world . . . 'tis the condition of your creation . . . The utility of living consists not in the length of days, but in the use of time."[1] Now, centuries later, the reality that life is finite, transitory, and therefore dear remains a taboo subject and certainly not a topic of social chit-chat over wine and hors d'oeuvres. Many of us are uncomfortable talking casually about death. Few realize that when we are born into this life, we come with a round-trip ticket. We spend our allotted time here, and then we leave. That departing trip is called death.

Often while writing, self-doubts arose and demanded to know why I was writing a book on death anyway, wondered if anyone would want to read it, and questioned its purpose. Sharing my thoughts, my friend said, "Don't worry about it. The purpose of any book lies in the hearts and minds of its readers." Of course, I thought. How simple. My concerns eased. As realization of death's sacredness grew, fears eased.

At times it seemed simple; birth and death frame varying and unknown durations called lifetimes. Birth is greeted with joy. Rarely does one hear the lament: *Oh! That poor woman. I hope her labor is not long.* No one exclaims: *That poor baby! What trials and hardships lie in wait for him? What heartbreaks will she have to endure?* We hear excitement about the birth of a baby. Death on the other hand is usually dreaded; its imminent arrival first denied and then accompanied by sadness or grief. We lose sight of death as natural passage for everyone.

Throughout history and geography, religions have treated birth and death as sacred events. Most religions embrace a version of the hereafter. Just out of the reach of consciousness, we hold a haunting ambivalence about death. With age, comes an acute awareness that life is a brief, indeterminate gift of time, too much of which is spent fearing death. The shamanic cultures say that in the West we have forgotten how to die, forgotten that we can consciously partake in the process, that we have lost our connection with the sacred significance of death. Freedom from fear of death resonates with the South American shaman and is evident in their Death rituals. Mourners and wise elders of the tribe join in shamanic death rites created to assist the dying in their journey to the other side. In contrast, Western culture attempts to artificially sustain life long after meaningful life is over.

The shaman's perspective of death is shared with the great thinkers of Europe. The German philosopher Martin Heidegger wrote, "If I take death into my life, acknowledge it, and face it squarely, I will free myself from the anxiety of death and pettiness of life... and only then will I be free to become myself."[2] Our reward for resolving our fear of death is a calmness that frees our energies to be spent on conquering the challenges of life and on experiencing life's richness. Ira Byock, a leading voice in educating the public about Western medicine's habit of keeping the hopelessly ill alive artificially, injects insight and knowledge into the harsh reality. His knowledge, kindness, and courage continue to re-educate the pubic in matters of our modern way of dying. In his book *Dying Well*, he wonders if the day will ever come when we will look back and understand that the "overwhelming fear of death has for so long covered up the fear of living."[3]

For many, the mere mention of death triggers feelings of uneasiness and discomfort. The thought of entertaining a different approach, one that includes an element of befriending death, is rare. We have much to learn about how we might address death, which indeed creates a challenging lesson. While many of us know that the most effective way for us to learn something is by doing whatever it is that we want to learn, however, one does not *do death* as a learning exercise. A person who has just died does not pop back over to our side where we can ask, "Hey, how did it go? What's it like, Buddy?" Actually, there is a great deal of information out there. In 1969, Dr. Elizabeth Kübler-Ross broke new ground in her candid book *On Death and Dying*, opening the way to begin conversations on death. In 1957, Raymond A. Moody, MD, wrote *Life after Life*. When his patients went into cardiac arrest and lost all signs of life, they would regain consciousness and share a similar story of moving through a tunnel toward indescribable light, beauty. They described an overwhelming sense of peace. A few were disappointed when they found themselves back here. While many scoffed at Moody's findings, his research continued. Today, near-death experiences are widely accepted and helpful in overcoming fear.

Current medical expertise enables us to revive people who otherwise would have died, making these experiences more common. There's a lot of interesting stuff out there to learn about. While people learn by doing, they also learn by observation and by gathering information, by self-reflection, and by modeling their behavior on the actions of others. We can learn, too, by going deeply into our own experiences, where seemingly inconsequential incidents carry lessons that open doors to expanding consciousness not only about living but also about dying. Insights and perspectives about death are within reach for all who seek them.

While writing about death, insights arose and fear looked me in the eye, demanding acknowledgement. Again and again, it brought me face-to-face with what I had not wanted to recognize, and doing so, taught me the beauty of finding deep comfort in the anticipation of my death. Death has extended its invitation several times, inviting me to come and dance death's dance. Each time, I have held my dance card close. Death waits, for death has reserved the last dance. I trust I will be ready when the invitation arrives and accept with grace and gratitude.

CHAPTER ONE

THE BOOKENDS: BIRTH AND DEATH

After years of sporadic, sometimes haphazard, and often tumultuous efforts searching for experiences of soul, I have learned little by little to trust my gut. Years ago, my gut feeling was that being alert and present during the births of my children was paramount. I wanted to touch life, to feel it, rub up against it, to breathe in the smell of it. I wanted to be alert when a new life emerged from my body. During the early 1950s, it was not uncommon for a sedated mother in the hospital obstetrics ward to be told the morning after childbirth whether she had given birth to a boy or a girl. In the early 1950s, no classes taught fathers how to coach mothers through labor. Fathers waited in waiting rooms so as not to disrupt the work of the doctors whose goal it was to do everything possible to avoid the mother's pain while delivering a healthy baby. It felt to me as though every effort was being made to remove the mother from the birthing process.

Suspecting pregnancy, I saw a doctor and cheerily volunteered my philosophies about childbirth. I wanted to be awake, but fearing the severe headaches that I had been told were side effects of having a spinal, I didn't want one. The doctor found the idea of being awake during childbirth without blocking the pain appalling. To top it off, I said that I planned to nurse my babies.

He admonished, "That's not the modern way. Today, mothers feed their babies Similac. It's a better product." He then advised me to dry up my milk as soon as possible so that my breasts wouldn't sag, adding an additional advantage—I wouldn't have the inconvenience of nursing. After offering succinct professional advice, he left the small examination room, explaining that he would be back to examine me. Lying on the examination table for what seemed like forever, legs high and wide in the cold metal stirrups, I felt vulnerable. Finally, the doctor returned, examined me, and confirmed that I was indeed pregnant. His words echoed through the small room. "I was pregnant. I was going to have a baby!" My excitement turned to concern. I explained that I had experienced spotting. The doctor said casually, "Well, if you want to keep the baby, you'll have to stay off your feet." That was impossible. I was teaching full time to put my husband through graduate school. The doctor shrugged. "That's what you'll have to do. You can get dressed now," he said as he left the room. Fortunately, the spotting soon stopped and was no longer an issue.

Although devastated by the doctor's attitude, I was not about to budge. I wanted to be conscious. I wanted to be involved in what was going on. This guy was definitely not going to be my doctor. I left his office fighting tears, got in the car, and sobbed all the way home. Once home, I became angry. I will not have a spinal. I will be awake and know what's happening. I will nurse my baby. I will find another doctor! Promptly opening the Yellow Pages to Physicians and Surgeons: Obstetrics and Gynecology, I started calling. Trembling with anger and feeling desperate and alone, I tried being calm and failed miserably. My near hysterical words ran together. "I'm pregnant and I want to be awake when I have my baby and I don't want a spinal and I want to nurse my baby. Does your doctor allow this?" Silence and then, "Can you hold please?" "Yes." I said.

While waiting on hold, I imagined their saying things like "This one sounds like a real loony. We do not want her here." Soon a nurse was back on the phone. Her polite but firm voice suggested that I seek another doctor. Maybe no doctor would want to deliver my baby. Thankfully, the list of doctors whose names began with an A was not long. By the time I started calling the doctors beginning with B, I had calmed somewhat and sounded more reasonable. Dr. Bach saved me. *No, he did not use spinals; yes, he encouraged breast-feeding. However, he would need to check and see if he had time available when I was due to deliver. Yes, he had time!* My short search was well rewarded. How blessed I was that his name began with B. If his name had been Williams or Yates, I doubt if I could have hung in there. In retrospect, I have wondered if my attitude would have shifted with my subsequent deliveries had the birth of my first child been long and difficult. Would I have opted for an alternate choice? I will never know, for luckily my labors were short and uncomplicated.

Marriage and motherhood filled my life. The consuming demands of a new baby girl were increased thirteen months later with the arrival of a baby brother. Three-and-a-half years, another little brother joined our family. Life found its rhythm. Thoughts of death did not enter my mind. Then came a phone call from my mother telling me about the death of one of her closest friends, and thoughts of death came rushing back. In college, I remembered telling a friend's mother how I felt about birth and death, and how I wanted to be there for both. The mother had been more than uneasy. She was shocked and embarrassed and scolded me harshly, telling me that I was too young to even think about such things and that my ideas were crazy. She was probably right. I really didn't know what I was talking about. They were just feelings I had.

Just as birth is an important mystery, so is death. We are born into life. Death is a birth of another kind. In death, we are being born out of life and into the next whatever comes after. When I mentioned my thoughts to a few others during that time period, they had been obviously ill at ease, which I was sure conveyed their disapproval. Ashamed and embarrassed, it was a long time before I said a word on either subject, although I continued to be drawn toward the mystery of it all. But that had happened years before. While I was sad to hear that Mama's friend had died, now was not the time for reflection. The kids were tired and fussy and demanded my attention. They needed to be fed and bathed and the baby put to bed. My husband expected his dinner to be ready when he came home. Ponderings on death would have to wait.

A few years later and over a period of about six months, several deaths among family members and close friends occurred one after another. The closeness we all shared compounded the impacts of their deaths.

Attending funeral after funeral and seeing many of the same grieving faces over and again created an eerie sense of collective suffering. Death's presence, thick and dark, enveloped us, deepening our pain and arousing our fears. First our neighbor died. He was in his early 70s and had not been well for many years, so his death did not surprise us. We were sad, but not devastated. In a month, another neighbor was killed in a car accident, leaving his wife and three teenage sons, boys I had babysat when they were toddlers. Our families were close. The shock of his death left us reeling.

Less than two months later, Matt, Marilyn's devastated husband, called me with the news that my friend of many years had uterine cancer. By the time symptoms arose, the cancer had metastasized. For the next five months, I made an extreme effort to be with every minute possible until she died. Her son was ten; her daughter, eight.

Our time of being together took us deep into the realms of the heart, of life, of death, things we had not shared before. Our closeness during her final months of life triggered thoughts about my own death. Marilyn, now a wraith of her former self, inspired me with her courage. Clearly the thread of life is tenuous. Several weeks after Marilyn's funeral, my older brother, Stafford, called. Paul was dying. "NO!" I sobbed into the phone. "No. No. No. I don't want for anyone else to die! I can't bear another death. Not Paul. Please, don't let it be Paul."

My brother was quiet for several moments and then said gently,

"I'm sorry. I know how much you're hurting, but Paul is in the hospital, and he's dying. I need to see him, and I need you to come with me."

All of us knew that Paul wasn't well, and we all had retreated into our shelters of denial. In our pain, we slowly faced reality. We were losing a beloved friend. I curled up inside myself trying to find a place that would allow me to give way to my numbness.

Entering the hospital room, I gasped. There, hauntingly thin and lifeless, Paul lay on an elevated hospital bed, tubes everywhere dripping food, medications, and painkillers into and urine out of his unresponsive body. Machines pumped air into his no-longer-functioning lungs and blood through his failing heart. Paul had been dynamic and vital. His laughter was contagious. He filled a room with vibrant energy. Seeing him now devastated me, and I suddenly felt light-headed and unsteady as my long-set-aside questions about death roared back. Clinging tightly to my brother's arm gave me a fragile sense of steadiness.

Nurses swarmed about the room, faces grim, attentions focused on checking dials and drips and blood-pressure cuff. No one touched Paul. The medical mechanics of saving a life consumed every molecule of energy available. But they were not saving a life, they were attempting to slow what they could not reverse, the inevitable onrush of death. Paul's death was now a medical situation. The patient was ignored, as was our presence. The essence of the person doing the dying placed a distant second in the hospital's priority system. Grieving family or friends didn't make the cut. Focus was on the frenetic effort to defeat death. That all attempts would be futile was clear.

Making a supreme effort to hide our agony, my brother and I stood by Paul's bed. I wanted to put my hand on his forehead. I wanted him know we were there. I wanted to tell him we loved him. As I cautiously reached to touch

Paul's forehead, a nurse firmly took my wrist, drawing my hand back, shaking her head, and whispering, "*No!*" Energy of desperation filled the hospital room. A nurse motioned to us to stand back. A doctor came in and looking directly at my brother and me standing against the wall, flicked his hand angrily toward the door. We left obediently. Abandoning Paul filled me with sickening guilt. Feelings of helplessness, loss, and pain joined my emerging anger.

Driving home, my brother sat stoically behind the wheel, eyes intent on traffic, mouth quivering almost imperceptibly as he blinked back tears. Sitting next to him, I burst out sobbing, my pent-up thoughts of death roiling up to fuel my hysteria. I kept repeating, "Paul shouldn't have to die like that. He is dying, and we just walked away and left him. It's wrong. Stafford, it is wrong! Marilyn didn't have to die like that. She had her family with her. She had her friends. I don't want to die alone like that. No one there even cared about Paul." I ranted on, imploring my brother to not let that happen to me. Although Stafford's suffering was palpable, I was absorbed by my own pain and fear and offered him no consolation. Oblivious to his anguish, I continued to bombard him with my relentless pleading. He was my big brother, an attorney. I counted on him to know what to do and not let me die as Paul had died. He took my verbal onslaught in silence.

At Paul's funeral, an unreal haze enveloped us. Neither my brother nor I was able to speak at the service. The loss of this man left an abyss, making us realize how huge he had been in our lives. The eerie coincidence of having so many people who were close to us dying all around us intensified and deepened our grief. After Paul's funeral, we drove to my brother's home. He pulled the car into the driveway, turned off the ignition, and sat silently for a few moments before turning to me. Speaking softly, he said, "I don't want to die like Paul had to die either." Never had I seen my brother bereft like this. Then he hugged me for the longest time.

"If you die first," I said, rushing in to solve the problem, "I promise that I'll do everything I can to make sure it won't happen to you. I don't want that to happen. Let's write it down, you know, how we feel about dying. Maybe then someone will listen."

I was telling him what I would do as though I knew what could be done. I did not.

"Yes, I'll do that, I'll have it written up at the office, all proper and legal. It's certainly worth a try." His voice was soft and his words tentative.

It was a long time before our grief eased and our mourning ran its course, but the horror of that hospital scene stayed with us, and little by little we were able to share more about how each of us had felt as we stood by helplessly, watching our friend die. In time, we realized that each of us there in that hospital room was a victim of an amalgam of good intentions, medical know-how, vast ignorance, and fear. Our conversations strengthened our resolve. Unfortunately, he never seemed to find the time for preparing our declaration, and it was never written.

Our lives continued, filled to the brim with marriages, families, friends, and careers. The joys and tragedies that beset all lives visited our lives as well. Routine pressures of our everyday living demanded whatever time and energy we had to give, leaving little space or inclination for thinking about how we were going to die at some unknown time in the future.

Decades later, my brother would die. Within weeks after his death, my day of reckoning came, unannounced. Memories of that ride home from the hospital flooded back to me, slapping at my insides, filling me with shame and regret. Fresh tears gushed. I wept in rueful memory of my brutal and selfish onslaught, demanding that my brother take care of me. I wept, too, as I acknowledged his devastating grief, and I wept because it was too late to tell him how much I loved him, and that I was sorry.

CHAPTER TWO
TURNING POINTS

Life moved forward, keeping step with most lives in the era and geography paralleling mine. Trying to live life to the fullest, to seek new dimensions of meaning, and to grow in whatever ways I could possibly grow continued to intrigue me. Yet I, as most of us, spent uncountable days plodding along, doing what had to be done. While life can often be wonderful, setbacks do occur. The ups and downs weave their ways through the muddle of the everyday, demanding their spaces and taking their tolls. Real tragedies entering our lives can move us beyond discouragement and into depression.

It didn't take major depression to find that life's meaning was nowhere to be found when I was already late, either stopped or inching along in stalled freeway traffic, or when someone backed into the side of my parked car and drove away with nary a note or contact number, or when I burned dinner just as guests were to arrive, or when the dog was sick all over the newly cleaned carpet. More troubling were the times when I felt judged or rejected, or when I failed to live up to my own expectations and was sure I had let someone down. From the picayune to the important, distractions filled my life and overwhelmed me just as they filled the lives of most of us. Life is made up of chaotic trivia as well as real stuff.

I remained stuck in the accepted 1950s mindset. A woman's job was to see to it that her husband's life was as stress-free as possible, an impossibility that plagued and defeated us. The man's priorities prevailed, a system supported by Society. When I decided to return for a master's degree, the advisor asked what degrees my husband had. "A bachelor's and a master's," I said. He said that I should wait until my husband got a PhD. It was not appropriate for a wife to have more education than her husband. Amazingly, it didn't occur to me to challenge this position. Further education waited until after I left my marriage and needed additional education in order to increase my income.

The routine necessities of daily life took center stage. Trying to figure out where to look for consciousness amid life's chaos brought challenges that exceeded my capacity to respond. Frustration would set in, followed by what I dubbed *terminal ennui*. Often, I was loath to recognize that this same demanding stuff proffered nuggets of insight. When I did and was able to step back and take a retrospective look at what had been going on, viewing it from a different vantage point, I realized that I had grown in major ways.

Aging helped, too. With age came new perspectives. Life eased up. Fewer situations were worrisome. After two decades, and when my children were in their teens, I left my marriage. A variety of interesting careers followed. Life had settled down. Kids were now grown and married with kids of their own. I moved back to my home state, where I designed and was owner-builder of a small cottage. With construction complete, magical gardens planted and thriving, I enjoyed writing, sculpting, and gardening, had a small clientele, and entertained friends. I basked in having time with my children and grown grandchildren. Things could not have been better.

Then my smoothed-out life became bumpy and caught me by surprise, made me uncomfortable and confused. There was no apparent reason for this upheaval, but in the spring of 2005, an all-consuming urge arose, invading my life with an uneasy pressure for me to return to school for a doctorate. My sense of logic was offended. My critical theorist made it clear that the very thought of earning a doctorate at this late stage in my life was nonsense. Doctoral studies would take an inordinate amount of my time, be one horrendous amount of work, and be unthinkably expensive. My logic chastened my intuition to quash this idiocy! To cancel it out! Be done with it! The rigorous work required held no appeal to me whatsoever. Actually, it made me shudder. Life was wonderful as it was. I had two degrees, which were all I would ever need. "Forget it," I found myself repeating aloud, often shaking my head and body as if to rid myself of this craziness. The urgings refused to leave. Instead, they intensified.

Each day moved me closer, and by June, unaware of any specific turning point, the decision having clandestinely seeped into my being, I began the application process by assembling over a half-century of transcripts from ten different schools. Then I began completing the application itself: Names of supervisors and/or employers. Hmmm. I had been self-employed for over forty years. Before that I was a stay-at-home mom. Before that, I taught school and doubted if any of the principals were still alive. Next: Career Goals: My multiple and varied careers were behind me, or so I thought. In spite of my diligent resistance, by the fall of 2005, at age seventy-six, I found myself enrolled in The Pacifica Graduate Institute to earn a PhD in depth psychology. Although I knew deep inside that Pacifica was the right place for me to be, my reasons for being there remained a mystery.

Perhaps it was because of Pacifica's emphasis on the work of Carl Jung. In my late twenties, depressed and suicidal, I found my way to Hilde Kirsch, who had taken her training from Dr. Carl Jung, and it was he who had designated her a Jungian analyst. This information was unknown to me at the time, making her credentials inconsequential in my admiration of her. I was impressed with her because our time together changed my life in a positive and deep way. The thought arose that maybe I was here at Pacifica so that I could integrate what I had learned through education, Jungian analysis, and life experience in general with the knowledge gained in the context of a formal and rigorous course of study. In a way, I felt as though I were coming home to set the capstone. However, with or without justification, I was at peace with my decision. Actually, I was more than at peace. I was intensely committed to and involved in the work that lay ahead.

The challenge was huge. In my mid-seventies, I was entering a five- to-eight year program that would cost approximately $100,000. It was obvious insanity. The first three years consisted coursework for three of the quarters, and a fieldwork project assigned for the summer. From two years to eight years were allotted for writing the dissertation. The one thing my logical self demanded was that I dedicate no more than four years to this crazy doctoral effort, which left me one year for dissertation writing. At the onset, the plan was to finish as I turned eighty.

My fellow students were significantly younger than I, and while we shared a feeling of camaraderie and held many views in common that allowed for our genuine appreciation of each other, decades of life experiences made clear that differences in perspectives do come with age. My short-term memory adamantly refused to work full time, spontaneously flitting off to places unknown when I needed her help. My focus, however, had intensified, my consciousness had become clearer, and my creativity flowed. I loved my white hair while I lamented the departure of my hearing and vision. My appreciation of the years lived had grown, as had my need to go to bed early. Old age, as with any age, has its gifts and its curses.

The program poured forth an abundance of information, wisdom, and insights, required long classroom hours, seemingly endless pages of reading, and numerous papers to write. Sitting in the front row, leaning forward, hands cupped behind my ears, I struggled to hear the instructors while depending heavily on reading their faces. Taking notes was a challenge. If I looked away from the instructor in order to write, I missed hearing the next sentence or two. Before starting the second year, I had purchased hearing aids.

Bit by bit, answers to questions about why I was on campus began to emerge. Psychological theories merged with current and remembered experience. Learning was being interwoven with what I had done or was doing in my life. Patterns appeared. New insights took up residence in my papers. Once again, I saw my life in a new light. Again, I recognized being actively involved in the individuation process, Jung's term for moving toward becoming all we can become, of moving toward wholeness. It requires that we look inward and own both our abilities and our fears as we explore the vast and dark unknown of the unconscious. In time, one learns to look inward for causes, insights, and solutions instead of looking outward for a culprit or scapegoat. Over time I learned not to squander the gifts that had come with me with my birth.

Pablo Casals said it perfectly. "I was born with an ability, with music in me, that is all. No special credit was due me. The only credit we claim is for the use we make of the talent we were given . . . What we do with our talent is what matters. You must cherish this gift."[4] In old age I can at last own and cherish my gifts, a state of mind that was being promoted and encouraged by my studies. As knowledge and insights were gained, a pattern developed. Early on in the program, I explored the possibility of finding a place in my dissertation for this pattern of what I began to think of as a series of increments of transformation.

In those exploratory stages, I was leaning toward looking at how ordinary life offers extraordinary examples of how we learn and grow; to show how Jung's Individuation Process takes place in all around us all the time. It is how we continue to learn and grow. On a phone discussion with my advisor, he suggested that it might be wise for me to narrow the scope and focus on a more specific time frame.

"Why not focus on the final stages of the individuation process, old age, and . . ."

Not hearing the last of the sentence, I waited, listening intensely. After a long pause, my advisor said, "This is an interesting silence."

"I'm waiting for you to finish the sentence," I told him.

"Old age and. . . ." He paused and then slowly and clearly said, ". . . d e a t h."

Another silence. I was taken aback and unsure about how to respond.

"Oh. Umm. OK. Yeah, that's great! Yeah, I'm comfortable with that. Yeah. Sure, that's great. Yes! Yes. I can do death." I was rambling. More silence. More uneasiness. "I have a *Do-Not-Resuscitate* notice on my refrigerator door," I blurted out, scrambling to demonstrate my support of his suggestion. During this conversation, another side of me was thinking about how much fun it was going to be spending the next year concentrating on getting old and dying. Oh, well. What I really needed was a topic that would make its way past the dissertation gatekeepers, and now I had one.

Following my advisor's suggestion, the focus would be on old age and individuation in the final stages of life. To make this clear, he suggested the inclusion of appropriate wording to depict the final stages of life. Resurrecting material that I had drafted on the transformative process, I now sprinkled it liberally with the vocabulary of old age: *old woman, decades of memories, elderly, last years, imminent or impending death.* I thought about using the word *dotage*, winced, and decided against it. The focus on old age had begun. I knew that, in addition to its many rewards, our final years exact their dues, but all in all, I'm okay with old age.

While my four-year stipulation stayed clear in my mind, the year spent writing the dissertation remains a blur. On August 29th, 2009, five weeks after my eightieth birthday, the oral defense of the dissertation was completed and approved, and the PhD granted. My kids, grandkids, cousins, and friends cheered me on. Although their praises felt great, none of the people I know who have doctorates, and there are many, waited so long to complete the doctoral process. The recognition given me was a bit like giving the Gold Medal to the person who finished the race last. But that was okay with me. Degree in hand, I was ageless.

CHAPTER THREE

THE ETERNAL NOW: THE SPACE BETWEEN

For years it seemed that I lived life at some indeterminable point in time and space that I did not understand. Reading P. L. Travers, I resonated with her words. "Between all points of opposites there is a point—but could we find it—of reconciliation."[5] Is this the point I seek? Is this the illusive *Now*?

Now. I am. It is. Not was or will be. I attempt to make the shift. The issue of my death arises often, and with it comes the feeling of urgency to understand and resolve the concept of *Now*, yet I fail to see the connection between the concept of *Now* and my death. How does this *Now* business relate to this book? In popular magazines and bestselling books, we are counseled to live in the present, yet the *Now* as both a point in time or concept escapes me. How do I live in the *Now* when I can't find it?

Again attempting to focus on *Now*—to zero in on the precise moment between past and future—I can discern no dividing point. Studying the movement of flickering leaves as they move in concert with the slight afternoon breeze, I find no space in which to insert my awareness of *Now*. Their movement is seamless. With total concentration, I turn my awareness to the formation of a thought. The thought takes shape through the words that create and express it, words spoken silently in my mind, only to have the beginning of the word find completion and move into the past while the remainder of the word waits in the wings of the future ready to take form. As future arrives, the *Now* of my life slips seamlessly by me as it flows into my past.

Is the *Now* that has constituted my life, my every breath, my every experience, an illusion? I want to capture it, freeze its image with the click of a camera, examine it with a magnifying glass, to see and comprehend this illusive nanosecond in enlarged detail. *Now* defies scrutiny. Drowning in insane nitpicking, I struggle to understand how others can *get it* while *it* continues to elude me. I feel foolish and frustrated not understanding something as simple as *Now*.

Then, one lovely sunny morning while I dally in my garden, *Now* becomes clear to me. This clarity arrives out of nowhere, and its arrival has nothing to do with the intense effort I had expended to find it. *Now* is suddenly simple. This clarity comes not from my mind. It shows up while I am focused on deadheading roses or tediously pulling weeds from the Irish moss, while I relax in the sun and soft breeze. For me it arrives as the timeless space-between, between past and future, between the movements of back and forth, between the breath in and the breath out, between knowing and not knowing. *Now* is vast and timeless, simultaneously imperceptible and omnipresent. It is not of time and yet is of all time. It is the indefinable and infinite space within which I live. It holds me as it has held me since my birth and will hold me until my death.

What had come to me with such clarity was not new, but it was new to me. Until we experience something, it is not completely real to us. Experience finds its way through to us in myriad ways, some directly and others vicariously. Being exposed to ideas or experiences and not connecting with them is common. When we do connect with a new awareness, that new truth seems to appear magically, and from that point on, is found in abundance. Have you ever noticed that when you learn a new word and understand what it means, it suddenly pops up everywhere? So it is with new insights. We continually receive and select information, all the while carrying within us a process for selective perception that edits out what we are unwilling or not ready to see. Yet, when the time is right, the unconscious will present its gift of clarity, allowing us to do *the work* we are ready for and need to do.

Memory ruptures the veil of time, allows experiences long past to come mysteriously alive again. Feelings, scents and sounds vibrate more rapidly. Colors intensify. Previous experiences emerge from memory and recreate themselves, oft times with more depth and richness than when the experiences first occurred. The interim years allow new dimensions and perspectives to become clear, endowing memory with enhanced meaning. An interconnection between memory and the current act of experiencing is an ongoing interweaving of eras and facets of a person's self and life. I breathe this clarity in and yield to it, allowing a flow of numinous clarity—one of many gifts that come more often in old age.

One role of memory is to hold one's unresolved stuff in place, in reserve, if you will, and when a propitious moment arrives, memory offers the salient stuff back to us. It is then that we can re-experience the mélange of both contents and feelings held in those memories and find new insights and fresh perspectives. Once seen, we can recognize the value of our pain that we had not seen before. Some memories are welcome, for they are rich in content, ready to be dissected and reordered. From this distance, new aspects show themselves, allowing for greater understanding. Incidents once seen one way now take on a new aura or persona or a different emotional body. Something once trivialized now holds meaning. Other memories are no longer necessary. I have checked them out. They carried little importance. It is time to weed the garden of my memory—to give thanks for lessons learned and then relegate them to the soul's compost pile, where they will transform into nourishment to feed renewal.

In memory as everywhere, there is continual dying and being reborn. Some facets of ourselves are finished and discarded. New insights and understandings are ready to be born and nourished. Birth, death, and rebirth create the flow that brings lavish gifts that we had neither seen nor understood before. To facilitate moving toward understanding, I have learned first to open to possibilities, allowing for conception and then leave it be. Gestation has its own timeline. Then I write. For me, writing is the midwife.

The finding of *Now* moves past and future to the periphery. The past is condensed and its components are instantly available on demand, sometimes by invitation and other times by intrusion. Chronological order no longer applies. Memories follow neither clock nor calendar. Content and relationship transcend time and erase distance as they bring together pieces of soul in the creation of both new consciousness and wholeness. Sequences of interrelationships, whether dressed in words or mental pictures, show a cohesive if not chronological pattern. The intense and undeniable interweaving of observed and observer or of subject and object is essential. In the transformative process through which we find ourselves moving closer to wholeness, the unconscious yields up the bounty of its contents via the pathways offered through memories.

Once those experiences are drawn back into the *Now*, they hold sway as they play out in brilliant detail, reenacting their original performance. In so doing they are again prime players in the *Now*. While some memories of old dialogs or experiences are invited and welcomed, there are others that barge in carrying unresolved emotional refuse that demands resolution or at least a serious examination. Memories offer a rich medium for the creation of consciousness.

Although the future holds plans, dreams, and ambitions as well as dread and fear of the unknown, routine days usually unfold as planned. School starts each fall on the date designated by the school district's board of education. We attend our local high school football game on Friday night as scheduled. The dental appointment for next Tuesday at 9:30 will most likely take place at 9:30 on next Tuesday. Certainty, however, is never possible. The past holds knowledge gained, wisdom earned, as well as experiences of life's ordinariness, its pain, regret, joy, excitement, and achievements. Discouragement, fear, suffering, guilt, and regret join a potpourri of contrasting emotions that are alive and well in memory, although they have lost their linear structure. Any one of them can be pulled into the *Now* at any time to be re-lived and perhaps reprocessed and restructured.

Living in the *Now* can be tricky. The superficial re-creation of our pasts that erases the hardships and the pain can tempt us, call us away from the challenging and difficult times of our present lives. The *Now* can be formidable. The pull to find an easier place to live is strong. Moving into the past and surrounding ourselves with altered and sugarcoated memories does not ease the longing of the soul to strive for wholeness and meaning. Setting our feet firmly in our fantasy past, we repeat our modern-day mantras. *Things just aren't the way they used to be. I remember the good old days when… Things are going to Hell in a hand basket* or *When I was a boy….* The essential *Now-ness* of our lives slips by, and eventually looking back we say, *If only….* As we wait to experience the *Now, Now* never comes. We lament *Maybe someday,* or *When I finish this project* or *When I get a different job.* The nebulous *Now* eludes us; we wonder why.

As I recall pain-filled memories, I experience again old fear-laden or anger-filled incidents. Then, if I revisit them in a new context of greater wisdom, knowledge, and understanding, the memories can shift, diffusing the pain and anger. Past-lived incidents are instantly available to the present to bring memories long-held until we are ready to reconfigure them, shifting perspectives and densities of emotions.

The future, too, has the power to call us away from our current struggles and our inability to cope with life's demands and challenges. When most of our weeks or days begin with the same *I have a new lead on a job coming through next week. I am working on a deal, and it's getting closer every day.* Holding a repeated conversation while waiting passively for our future to arrive allows the future to rob us *of Now.* Living in a never-arriving future leaves our present lives filled with a gnawing sense of emptiness.

The defining lines are blurry. When is living in the future an escape? When is it a way of visualizing our future dreams into being and move in rhythm with our ever emerging and changing lives? Are we able to separate our ability to mine the treasures found in memories from living in the past? Questions to be pondered. Embracing the *Now* helps us stay grounded as we prepare for a death without fear. As we move along the continuum of life, the past grows as a resource from which to draw as our futures diminish. Appreciation of life and acceptance of death together create peace, while providing a stability that holds us steady as we move through a healing resolution of fear. What is no longer feared no longer needs to be hidden. Resolving fear allows death to come out of its hiding place deep within the recesses of our denial. Out in the open, it can now be greeted and accepted, and defused, clearing the way for us to prepare the psyche for the final leg of this physical lifetime. *Now* is when we re-form and re-create as we dream a peaceful death into being. How fitting that *Now-ness* tugs at me for acknowledgement just as I move irrevocably into the reconciliation of my own death.

As I reach to embrace the vast and un-embraceable *Now*, I find it colored by both future and past; yet as rich as the past has been or the future might become, both take a back seat to the excitement and urgency of living through the final *Now* of our lives.

Knowing that *Now* hides in the infinite nanosecond between moving up and down, between forward and backward, I watch the pendulum of my grandmother's clock with a new fascination. With a new wonder, I witness my breath as I inhale and exhale. The nanosecond of *Now* is at the same time the ever-present infinite space within which life takes place. Without experiencing the *Now* in everyday living, how would I be able to be present so that I could live in the *Now* of my death? For it is in the *Now* of our lives that death, too, takes place.

CHAPTER FOUR

AGING GRACEFULLY WESTERN STYLE

For the most part, people want to live long lives, which requires living many years, and thus creating a conundrum. To live for many years, a person must age, yet no one wants to get old. The only way one can succeed in not getting old is to die young, an event that removes the possibility of living a long life. To complicate matters, fear of dying is often hidden under a fear of aging, which contributes to our view of old age as a scourge. Living to a ripe old age while staying somewhere between thirty-five and forty-five is not something modern technology has nailed down to date. Staying young has become a national obsession, joining the obsessions of being thin and staying happy. With effort, one can achieve being slender, however, staying happy all of the time is an unreal expectation, and putting a hold on aging is out of the question. One can stay healthy, but that doesn't stop the clock.

Old age and our excess weight have more in common than being listed on our drivers' licenses. Society is telling us that to be old and fat is not a good thing. However, whether or not we add pounds with time, each year we are a year older. Age and weight are frequently discussed topics consuming an inordinate amount of attention and concern. Both invite an array of impossible or primarily ineffective solutions. Take heart. Aging with a degree of health, a modicum of wisdom, an accepting attitude, and a smattering of vitality and grace is possible.

In Western culture we are continually cautioned not to age. Headlines on magazines at checkout stands display bold titles: *Stop Aging! Turn Back the Clock! Miracle Treatment Takes Years Away! Be Young Again!* Television screens are cluttered with advice on how not to get old. Marketing strategies have cleverly connected aging gracefully with hiding the outward signs of aging, and indeed when we think we look better, most of us do feel better, but feeling better about how we look does not buy us more years. Feeling good might make the years we have more pleasant. Today's messages imply that eternal youth is available for the price of a product or surgical procedure. Enjoy beauty but don't confuse beauty with living a long time. Everyone ages. As one turns fifty, it is safe to assume that the following birthdays will herald in age fifty-one and then fifty-two. Fiftieth birthdays are not followed by birthdays forty-nine and forty-eight, no matter many miraculous face-creams one uses. Aging is stopped only by death. Those of us who are old are the lucky ones. But getting back to our attempts not to get old, a new arena has opened to us.

While many members of the dental community have not been caught up in pushing expensive, cosmetic procedures, some have joined the pharmaceutical and medical communities in their frenzy to sell remedies and procedure to make us more confident about how we look. The implications include making us look younger, and if we look younger, we might just convince ourselves that we are not getting old. We associate beauty with youth, but do perfect teeth truly defy age? Having one's teeth whitened is an innocuous enough procedure. Dazzling white teeth are becoming the norm. The pressure to get veneers and braces in marginal situations is on the increase and at times does not represent good dental care. I am in my eighties. My upper teeth are reasonably straight, my bite is accurate, but the bottom teeth have always been crooked. No one ever sees them, so they have never bothered me. Recently, in a video taken during a speech I was giving, I noticed that crooked lower teeth were beginning to show, and one offending tooth piqued my vanity.

When I asked the dentist what might be done, he explained that, in old age, the face sags so the lower teeth show—not very heartwarming information. Anybody past thirty already knows that everything is beginning to sag, and those of us in our late years know that everything has already done so. The dentist advised a full set of braces to bring the lower teeth into alignment, and, of course, the upper teeth would need adjustment to match the now-realigned lower teeth. The cost: five to seven thousand dollars! The time involved would be from three to five years. I imagined myself lying in my coffin with a full mouth of braces protruding through my shrunken and sagging lips and began to laugh. Later, an implant to replace the front tooth I knocked out in a nasty fall—a tooth worth replacing—was in the final stages of installation. As the dentist and I were both concerned about the color match, he took time to point out that my gums had receded and the teeth were darker at the top and offered that he could fix that. How? I asked. "Veneers," he replied. Hmmm, I wondered and then asked, "What are veneers and what do they cost?"

The dentist stepped back away from the dental chair. His assistant immediately sat down by my side and opened a book containing photographs showing horribly disfigured mouths now made beautiful. The changes were amazing! I could appreciate how the lives of these individuals have been transformed. My teeth, however, looked nothing like the photos in the sample book. No one has ever taken me aside to tell me to do *something* about my smile. The office manager magically appeared and presented a cost breakdown of six-to-seven thousand dollars. I was stunned! One thing was for sure! I was not going to have veneers. At the time, I had an eighty-one-year-old mouth. My vanity had been given a reality check. If I needed an up-lift of any kind, I would take a trip to Paris! In the meantime, I would live with the imperfections of aging, including my receding gums and wrinkled face.

However, when I found different dentist and asked her about the tooth, she checked the x-rays, saw there was plenty of enamel, and explained that she could file the tooth down in fifteen minutes if I would like her to do that. "The charge?" I asked. "No charge," she said.

Intense focus on keeping wrinkles at bay may be the fear of death masquerading as a pseudo passion for eternal youth. Does it camouflage some vague hope that, if one doesn't look old, one might be able to postpone dying? The message is both powerful and profitable. It is important to realize that cosmetic procedures, whether by dentists or plastic surgeons, do correct physical characteristics that, if left as they are, can cause one to feel self-conscious or ashamed or unattractive. Surgery can be life changing in a positive way. It will not, however, stop a person from aging.

If some characteristic about yourself brings you great angst, look into having the problem remedied. If your nose takes up more than its share of your face, or if you just can't stand the shape of it, have it changed. If you have a wart on your chin, have it removed. Crooked teeth are straightened, and one feels free to smile. Straightened teeth also improve one's ability to chew properly. Teeth that are missing or have been destroyed by illness or acid can be made whole. Depending on the depth of our personal insecurities, these changes can often but not always make us feel better about ourselves. Yet in all too many cases, extensive plastic surgery leaves people as insecure and unhappy as they were before having the surgery.

Wanting to look and feel good is common, normal, and healthy. I believe that the vast majority of women—and a significant number of men—are either openly vain or in the closet about their vanity. It feels good to wear clothes that flatter the body. When hair and makeup are in order—marvelous! Taking care of oneself is one of many ways of valuing oneself. I wonder what would happen if the approach to beauty shifted, and instead of trying to look young, we tried to look healthy, vital, interested, and engaged in our lives. Must youth be our only yardstick for measuring beauty or social acceptability?

Remember that while we look better, and looking better feels wonderful, we are neither younger nor will we live any longer by making cosmetic changes. Our inherited genetic make-up can gift us with a long and healthy life. Living a healthy life-style can add years to our lives. Staying healthy is less exciting than the possibility of finding a modern-day fountain of youth. We are bored hearing about eating right and exercising. Both involve discipline, hard work, and the feeling that we are denying ourselves delicious goodies. Being healthy lacks excitement. *Ten New and Exciting Ways To Prepare Brown Rice* doesn't grab our attention. Chocolate tofu pudding with granola topping doesn't hold a candle to chocolate mousse topped with whipped cream, fresh raspberries, and a splash of Gran Marnier. Although taking care of ourselves can make us feel younger and better about ourselves, no one can actually turn back the clock. However, the idea of quick miracles to keep us young is sexier and plays better than the idea of staying healthy. Staying young plays a whole lot better than getting old. I have not seen any magazines at the checkout counters with the headline *Old Age Is the Greatest!* The advertisers know what they are doing. The dreams and illusions of staying young sell the magazines that advertise and write endlessly about products promising eternal youth and beauty. Sales carry the day!

Staying healthy enables the positive aspects of aging to be maximized and the downside of aging to be ameliorated. It is possible to live longer by taking care of oneself, but that is not the message being broadcast. The message we get is that once we start aging, any shred of a dignified, full, exciting, and sexy life is gone! Do not believe it! Many find life in their 70s, 80s, and 90s to be full and exciting, difficult and challenging, fun, and rewarding much like all of the other stages in life, except that now we have perspective and wisdom, making the ups and downs of life easier to navigate.

When we choose a healthy lifestyle and lose weight by changing how we eat and live, we are told that our *real age* is significantly less than our *listed age*. The good news is that if we continue to take care of ourselves, we might live longer as well as look and feel better than we would have otherwise. But don't be fooled. Our *real age* is the one on the driver's license that shows the time lapse between the date of birth and the present. We may look and feel younger because we are healthier, but headlines hawking good health sell fewer magazines.

Again and again, we hear the comment that *age is just a number*. Recently, there was a clip on television of a ninety-three-year-old woman who danced magnificently! The tag line read: *Age is Just a Number!* Nonsense. The video was sensational, not because this woman was a beautiful dancer—the world is full of beautiful dancers. The excitement involved her being ninety-three and dancing beautifully. Her age was the significant factor. Age is not just a number! Age is *the number!* It tells us how long we have lived. It is a marker of how much of our lives we have spent. It defines our lives as finite. The number of years we have for living our lives, although unknown, is limited.

One's age determines one's era. I was born in 1929, a couple of months before the disastrous financial crash that plunged the country into the Great Depression. My childhood was spent in the 1930s, and frugality was ingrained into my psyche. December of 1941 signaled the start of WWII. I remember roller-skating on the neighbor's long concrete walkway—the only one in the neighborhood—when the news came. We were at war—a war that ended in 1945, and deeply influenced my teenage years. My children, born in the 1950s, are *baby boomers* and grew up in a completely different environment than the one of my childhood. The children born now and in the future will experience a level of social complexity and technological sophistication undreamed of in my lifetime. The era in which one is born leaves its defining and indelible impressions. Age matters.

As I begin researching how one might manage the process of aging, followed by old age itself and the undeniable reality of impending death, it occurs to me that I am already old and have already addressed many of those issues. What if this formal study on getting old reveals that there is a right way and a wrong way to do it? What if I find that I have done it all wrong? It is not something one can go back and do over. It is a disconcerting thought. Will I regret not exploring the eternal-youth business being offered by numerous publications on the market? I don't think so, but I don't know.

When people tell us we don't look old, we understand that they mean it to be a compliment. Is it a way of denying old age, avoiding acknowledgment of an undesirable stage of life? The implication appears to be that it is okay to be old as long as you do not look old and never, ever acknowledge being old. Let me interject that I am old! At times, old age receives treatment similar to the treatment given Lepers a century or so ago. However, with baby boomers by the thousands stepping into the arena of old age, new attitudes about aging are coming into play. Looking good holds its place in our priority system, but more and more people are actively staying healthy and involved.

Senior organizations abound. Although questions remained unanswered, numerous others are finding answers. Acceptance that our lives are finite and death is final is opening doors to an appreciation of living our lives each day. We can study and listen and learn in our later years just as we have always done. All stages of life include joys, troubles, challenges, and satisfactions. There is no question that old age has its share. Our bodies thicken and sag; the jaw line loses definition; the face wrinkles and falls. In spite of this, middle and old age do not deserve the bad rap they receive. Many have the tendency to look back on earlier days and embellish our pleasant memories while allowing the sharpness of painful memories to lose their edge in an attempt to ease the pain and enable brutal traumas to fade.

Teenage years can range from awful to catastrophic. We feel isolated and ignored and want to be popular and loved. We may love our parents and hate their rules and restrictions. Young-adult years are often filled with the stress of raising children with too little money, too little knowledge, and too little time to do the job. Marriages that were exciting when they were fresh begin to unravel as stresses of life settle in. Mid-life commonly finds married couples caught up in diverging interests and in separate ruts. The demands of ailing parents-now-grandparents are staggering. Elderly parents needing care on one side and rebellious teenagers challenging their parents on the other add new pressures to already-strained marriages in our middle-age years. Empty nesters are both free and lonely. No stage of life is without drawbacks. In spite of them, we manage to weave exciting and rewarding times into our lives. Old age, while treated as an affliction to be avoided, offers the potential for great peace of mind, of new perspectives and wisdom, as well as the now-free time available to pursue some of those long-denied creative talents. In spite of the pressure to stay young, we all age, even healthy people, and not surprisingly, feel much the same as we have always felt. Through every age, we take ourselves along.

Retracing steps, in 1949, my new marriage began as many marriages do, in a haze of euphoria. In 1949, six weeks after my twentieth birthday and three weeks after my wedding, I stood before thirty-six ten-year-old fifth graders at Lincoln School in Redondo Beach, California. I felt so grown-up. I was their teacher! They called me, Mrs. Ellis! My salary was $2,700 a year! I was absolutely sure I knew everything. No longer. In the *Now* of my late-in-life years, what I know for sure is that what I've learned over a lifetime is at best a microcosm of what is there to be learned. From the beaches of knowledge of this planet, I hold maybe a fist full of sand. We are wiser at fifty than at thirty-five, at sixty-five than at fifty, and wiser yet at eighty. Time does not make us a different person. It allows us to grow into our potential, while we remain ourselves. This *being ourselves* will carry us through our endless number of life experiences, and in spite of the pressure to not get old and die, we age and we die. For "do we not all swing between the poles of confidence and fear, collaborating with necessity?"[6]

Life is life at all ages. The *who-we-are-ness* brings a perspective that can help us stop wasting our lives on worrying about getting old. If we're fortunate, we will get old. We will be even more fortunate if we are healthy while this *getting-old* business is happening.

CHAPTER FIVE

ALIENATION FROM THE NATURAL

Discomfort with the word *death* leads to the use of euphemisms such as *She passed away last Sunday* or *He is gone now* or *Sadly, our friend Mary Beth has left us.* As a teenager I wrote a sympathy note at my mother's behest to express condolences to her friend, whom I liked immensely and whose husband had recently died. I wrote that I was sad to hear of her husband's death. I signed, sealed, addressed, stamped, and mailed the note. Immediately, I was gripped with sickening regret for having used the word *death*. I should have used the word *passing*, but I didn't. *His passing* would have sounded better or kinder than the word *death*. My insensitivity haunted me. Would the grieving widow be upset with me? Would she still like me? Would my mother find out what I had written and be disappointed in me? Those feelings remained vivid in my memory for years. Today, we have newer euphemisms to cushion the blow. *Crossing over* and

Entering the Hereafter are popular terms to soften what we perceive as death's harsh reality. Our denial of death fits logically and comfortably into today's far-reaching disconnect from the natural processes of life and of death. We as a nation, and quite likely as a part of a broader world society, generally deny aging and fear death. In our Western culture, as opposed to numerous other cultures, the once-venerated status of our elderly has been cast aside. The wisdom gained from years of experiences is no longer valued. Traditions once held and carried forward by our elders no longer play a role in our fast moving, technological society.

Our collective veneration is reserved, not for the elderly, but for the young. We sing our paeans to the young and work diligently to make youth reflect our ideal of perfection. The slightest flaws are deftly airbrushed away from already near-perfect bodies and faces of models in magazine ads. Television shows perfect people using perfect products to achieve perfect results. Whether the makeup we use or the food we buy, the image is perfection. Our artificially created ambiance has no warts anywhere.

Women and girls compare themselves to those bodies *sans* cellulite and faces without wrinkle, blemish, or pore and have learned to reject their own faces and bodies, a rejection that insidiously finds its way into our psyches, where it manifests in a Machiavellian form of self-rejection. Pre-teen girls attempting to emulate the gaunt-faced, bone-thin models of fashion's runways go on diets to lose either nonexistent baby fat or the chubbiness or obesity resulting from playing too many video games while munching too much fat-filled fast food. Twenty-year-olds have regular Botox injections to whisk away the first inklings of the inevitable wrinkles of aging. If we are not perfect because we do not look perfect, how can we expect to be worthy? Logically, we know that perfection is not possible. Our emotions pay no attention to that logic. The fantasy of perfection holds power over us and is the new scourge, decimating our ability to value of ourselves and wasting a huge amount of time, money, and energy.

This desire for perfection is endemic in Western society and is reflected in our disconnection from the natural world. Farm-raised salmon is artificially colored and lacks the Omega 3 found in wild salmon. Steaks and chops are neatly packaged, sometimes with a sprig of parsley or a slice of lemon. No dying, bellowing, bloody cattle are anywhere near today's immaculate meat counters. Our milk is bottled or boxed. After a field trip to a local farm, one second-grade boy from a suburban elementary school spoke out, his voice full of annoyed disapproval. *"Do you know where they get their milk? They squeeze it out of a dirty old cow. Don't they know they can buy it at the store in bottles?"*

Death, too, has been sanitized. While most of us want to die at home among friends and family, seventy-five percent of us still die in institutions and will likely continue to do so.[7] In those institutions, the dying are often recipients of distressing, painful, and even violent attempts to keep their hearts beating and their lungs taking in air, efforts that may result in prolonging life a few hours, days, or weeks, or a few months. The costs are staggering, not only in human suffering at a most vulnerable time of life but also in the unbelievable financial cost of today's health care delivery systems. "Medicare paid $50,000,000,000 [for care during] the last two months of patients' lives, more than the budget for the Departments of Homeland Security or Education,"[8] and "Although Medicare spending per terminal patient varies widely, [it was found that] higher spending does not result in longer lives or better deaths."[9]

Similar costs are involved in the attempts to resuscitate a cadaver, and when there are no Do-Not-Resuscitate orders on file, hospital policies generally require that all efforts be expended to prevent death, efforts that can continue for an hour or more after a person has died.[10]

Once a physician confirms death, another common hospital policy is to require that the family leave the bedside of their loved one within two hours.[11] The processing of the cadaver must begin. The bodies of the dead are covered, swept silently down the hospital freight elevators, and transported to the lab for autopsy or to funeral parlors where, amid soft music and artistically arranged flowers, the bodies are prepared for display on beds of satin in ornate caskets, hair beautifully coiffed, make-up perfect, and mouths clamped shut. No cries of pain or the disturbing sounds of the last rattling breath. No gaping mouths of the dead. No all-day gathering of family and friends keeping vigil. No time to comfort one another during those hours immediately after death. Many of us no longer feel equipped to deal with the dead and are relieved that professionals prepare Auntie Mae for burial.

Death fascinates us and draws us in while at the same time it repels us. This fascination is evident in our desire to witness multiple, vicarious exposures to violent death or threats of death. Watching programs depicting murder has become a popular form of entertainment that verges on morbidity. Books, movies and TV offer us safe venues and vantage points from which to observe death. Responding to this intense interest in violence and the need to increase viewers while filling a twenty-four-seven schedule, news programs contain an abundance of raw and brutal footage. In addition, our children spend untold hours playing violent video games featuring non-stop brutality, where attacking and killing each other is all a game, and where no one is really injured and no one really dies, furthering the disconnection between life and death. Thus tended to, a person's need to acknowledge and accept the inescapable fact of dying can remain dormant.

Many feel helpless around death and dying, and helplessness makes us uneasy. People we know to be grieving sometimes keep up a façade of cheeriness, as though not showing feelings minimizes the reality of their pain. Even if we, too, are grieving, we often join mourners by also hiding how we feel. Trivial chatter unsuccessfully attempts to hide meaningful conversation. We pretend when there is no need to pretend. All sadness and grieving are brushed out of sight but are never out of the real energies that fill the room. We shy away from the idea of dying or being in the company of someone who is terminally ill. At the same time, we suffer inside because we do not know what else to do but shy away. We feel deep within ourselves that we have somehow failed. In ignorance and uneasiness, when people come face-to-face with death, they find themselves incapable of action and withdraw.

In the 1970s, a high school student I knew was diagnosed with leukemia, which was at that time a death sentence. However, a new treatment had recently become available. The doctors referred to her as their miracle patient because she was their first teenage patient to receive this new treatment—and she got well. She grew up, married, had two children, and enjoyed both a successful marriage and a career. While in treatment, she shared with me the loneliness she felt when students, often including her friends, ignored her, walked past her, and pretended not to see her. She told me, too, that she understood that they were afraid to die, and being with her made them face the reality of death.

Evidence demonstrates that our medical culture avoids end-of-life issues in dealing with patients and with bereaved family members.[12] Medical personnel often announce death in a removed and professional manner and then leave the room.[13] Aloofness hides discomfort and contributes to the sense that dying is no longer part of the business of living. The failure of medical schools to provide courses on competent, let alone superior, care for dying patients exacerbates the suffering of families whose loved ones die in institutions. Few medical schools include courses on palliative care or on the dynamics surrounding both the dying person and the bereaved family and friends.[14]

In his informative book *Death Rights*, Stephen Kiernan shares research showing that the administering of a multitude of treatments to an individual who cannot be cured is a waste of medical knowledge and money. Although the amount spent on the last days and weeks of a person's life has no correlation with living longer or experiencing a calmer and more comfortable death, no expense is spared.[15] In the current Western medical paradigm, which is to diagnose, treat, and cure, death can be and often is considered to be a medical failure. When the doctor's sole job is to cure, death is not an acceptable option. The other extreme from providing excessive and invasive care to a dying individual is to do nothing. Patients have been ignored or abandoned, receiving only occasional or cursory attention as they await the inevitable.

As Baby Boomers care for aging parents, the need to face their own deaths becomes real. Concern rises about today's methods of dealing with death. More people are wondering if perhaps there is not a better way. With the largest number in history facing death over a relatively short period of time, the issue of how we address death calls for attention. It is time to reassess the appropriateness of the intense, invasive measures we inflict on those in their final days and hours.

Plans need to be laid out long before individuals reach the last critical stage of life. Medical interventions can work miracles, and pulling out all the stops is often necessary. Doctors, medical staff, family, and patient are rewarded with the patient's full recovery and extended, active, normal life. Even when recovery falls short of what the medical community and patient had hoped, a fulfilling life can be possible. On one hand, our appreciation of having the miracles of modern medicine there for us is huge. On the other hand, medical errors in prescribing prescription medication and in administering an excessive number of treatments are among the leading causes of death in this country.

In a 2012 article for the New York Times, Dr. Sanjay Gupta reported, "A reasonable estimate is that medical mistakes now kill around 200,000 Americans every year."[16] In spite of this, hospitals can be an appropriate place to be treated and made well. Hospitals are not good places to die.

When there is knowledge among the medical staff and family that someone is in the final throes of life—is in the actual process of dying—and when there is no possibility of reversing the irreversible coming of death, invasive and often violent and painful and frightening treatments are not called for. The person who is dying deserves a kinder and more peaceful place to be, where appropriate care is provided by those who are trained to work with the dying and honor death as the sacred passage out of physical life. We continue to hear about and read about family members commenting that prolonged suffering is not what the parent, friend, or relative would have wanted. There are actions to take to see that a person's wishes are honored and that grieving family members are not faced with making those painful, wrenching decisions.

When death does occur, as death eventually does, the doctor must state the cause of death on the death certificate, a practice that furthers the impression that death is a medical situation rather than a natural part of everyone's life.[17] When a person who is 103 dies in her sleep, most state and local statutes do not allow the cause of death to be natural causes or old age. "Actuaries seem unable to accept a natural cause of death as a cause of death. Cause of death must fit neatly into a distinct and clearly spelled-out classification."[18] In order to enter the records of the officially deceased, the dying cannot just finish up with the business of living, give out in old age, and cross over into the spiritual realm. Heart failure is a commonly listed diagnosis, and who can argue that the heart has indeed failed. Even a healthy heart wears out. This diagnosis of disease causing death adds to the implication that, if the disease had been treated properly, the death would not have happened. Never mind that not all illness is curable, or that our bodies wear out, or that death awaits us all.

Changes in our approach to death are simmering everywhere. The eight to ten thousand baby boomers reaching retirement age every week is serving as a catalyst to overhaul the dynamics around our attitudes toward death and dying. The runaway costs of our health-delivery system are waving red flags everywhere. Change is urgent.

Throughout the country, attitudes about death are shifting, and statutes are being rewritten to include *natural causes* as a legal cause of death. Our attitudes are moving toward accepting death as a natural phenomenon. That we cannot afford to wage war against the inevitability of imminent death and win becomes clearer. This statement does not mean that we shouldn't use all the medical knowledge, medications, and mechanical tools available to save the lives of those who have a chance at recovery. When a patient has appendicitis, medical know-how fixes the problem. If one has a heart attack or stroke, chances are that medical science can treat the condition and make continued years of productive life a reality. Improvements in medical care have resulted in some cures for cancers that were once considered incurable, although there remain cancers for which there are no cures. This book addresses those in the terminal stage of life, a situation understood by the medical professionals in charge of their care. Here, in the process of dying, comfort and love are the order of the day. Many who have suffered the painful ravages of illness are now victims of futile, frightening and painful treatments that do nothing but cause more misery. Death is the time to honor the needs of the dying and the grieving family.

As an exercise of the imagination, what if we were to view death as an honor that must be earned. We could not die unless we had lived our lives fully, given of ourselves generously, and courageously stood firm for things fair and just. Imagine having to continue aging, our bodies and minds slowly deteriorating, unable to be free of life's struggles. Imagine looking forward to a graceful departure after a life richly lived. This highly improbable shift in our society's view would certainly upset the current paradigm on death! We can all relax. Death will come to the worthy and unworthy alike. Addressing and accepting that reality will help break the chokehold that fear of death has on so many.

There are those who are at peace as death nears, free of fear and ready to die. Strong faith inspires many in their acceptance and comfort with death. Others never release fear's grip. Many walk each day with death, open to what the dying can teach them. Experiencing the deaths of others close up has heightened the reality of my own death, while at the same time, intensifying and expanding my appreciation for life. Sunsets are more vivid, families dearer, friends closer. I visit my death often, mentally, emotionally, and spiritually. In my eighties and healthy,

I could die tomorrow or twenty years from now. For me, meaning comes not from how long I will live, for death comes when it comes, but how I will continue to live, something over which I can exert some influence. For me, the question is not when I die, but how I live until I die and how I die.

CHAPTER SIX

FLIRTING WITH DEATH: PRACTICE RUNS

Standing eye-to-eye with old age and noting the changes in our physical bodies, the proximity of death becomes abundantly clear. When we're old and getting older, the logical next step is to die. Although individual lifetimes vary, aging and dying is a universal phenomenon. Death usually occurs in old age, but it can come at any time. An ever-increasing number of individuals find that their old age is followed by older age, but let's face it; we do not continue to get older forever. We eventually die—all of us. During our late-in-life reviews, when we look back on our multiple and varied experiences, it will become clear that we have had ample opportunities to come to grips with death and to see it as the natural and sacred process that it is.

As I moved through my seventies and into my eighties, it became imperative that I address this final act of living. Currently, I am doing the getting-old part of my life and will be doing the dying when its time comes, realizing, of course, that my death could come at any time. Its pending presence allows a more relaxed familiarity much like the comfort that comes when one gets to know someone whom they had feared and judged from a distance. Fear and judgment have a way of dissolving as we get to know a person. Old age also allows for greater acceptance of death's impending invitation, an emotional state that enhances the appreciation of day-to-day living. When we examine our lives carefully, the majority of us have lived arduous as well as rewarding lives, and many of us have experienced what we call near misses or brushes with death. Most of us can recall times when, had circumstances not been changed ever so slightly—a rescheduling of plans, a missed or cancelled flight, a sudden swerve to avoid a collision—we could easily have been injured, or we could have died.

Although our lives could have ended then and there, they did not. When we look at such incidents directly and honestly, we realize that death walks with each of us every day. Juan Carlos said often that death is an arm's length away.[19] Yet we continue to push away the idea of death. We stow our thoughts and fears of death with our other denials and continue to be oblivious of their sources. Those fears can be transformed into phobias, which we then empower. We plan our lives around their potential for causing us harm. Although for the most part, our daily lives go according to our plans, all of us know that the future remains a mystery. As diligently as we plan our lives, we never know all that life holds for us including how a person's death will unfold.

For years, the idea of dying while asleep held appeal. Later, with the consciousness of death as being part of life, I realized the value of being able to prepare myself to move comfortably toward and into death. During my 20s, I actually imagined my death, sort of a trial run. That death fantasy also served a purpose, although I was not aware of there being a purpose or that my fantasy death was a means of resolving issues that I could not consciously address. Feeling caught in a marriage from which I saw no possibility of escape, death fantasies served as a comforting way out. In the 1950s and 1960s divorced women were pariahs. No one in my family had ever been divorced. My vows included *Until death do us part.* Obviously, death was the logical solution.

My initial death fantasies were lovely and resembled those depicted in the old black-and-white films of the 1930s and 1940s. They were emotional and dramatic. The setting was a tastefully appointed bedroom with an elegant canopy bed. I lay there on my deathbed, propped among satin pillows, beautifully coiffed, and my makeup flawless. My beloved family and my dearest friends filled the room. Everyone had tears of sadness running gently down their faces. There was no noisy sobbing or blubbering or wailing or blowing of noses. Clearly, I was much loved. I sighed softly and was gone, just the way it was in the movies.

Today, I cringe and laugh at the unreal drama of it all. My actual encounters with death that threatened but did not materialize told different stories. As is true with many people, I have dallied and played tag with death several times over my lifetime, and those incidents were nothing like my movie-like fantasy death. I was not beautifully coiffed. No one wept at my bedside.

When I realized what lay beneath my less-than-virtuous death fantasies, they ceased. Giving them up did nothing to clear their underlying motivation, so I promptly replaced them with fantasies of my husband's untimely death in an accident. If he were a bit late coming home, thoughts of his death kicked in. Widows, after all, were looked upon with sympathy. If I, a young mother with three precious children, were widowed, that would provide a solution to my getting out of my marriage; plus I would be the recipient of everyone's love and sympathy and the life-insurance money. So removed was I from those self-serving thoughts that I actually cried as I mourned the loss of my husband, wallowing in tearful thoughts of his demise. I did it all, the funeral, everything, totally unaware of the genesis of my fantasy. Finally realizing the motivation for my charade, I was ashamed and grateful that no one had any inkling that I was fantasizing such things. I stopped playing with death wishes and addressed my marriage, which ultimately ended in divorce. Leaving my marriage took more courage that anything I had ever done, and while members of my extended family scorned my action, over the next few years they lined up like followers of the Pied Piper as one couple after another called it quits.

But let me turn back to the business of brushes with death. On one venture into the hallowed halls of a hospital, dye was injected into my veins in preparation for x-raying the function of my kidneys. I lay on the x-ray table trying to follow the technician's instructions given from his position behind a glass enclosure. *Take a deep breath and hold it.* I complied. *Good* he encouraged. The voice faded as the instructions continued. There was no longer a need for me to breathe. Suddenly, the gurney wheels clacked on the floor as two people, one on each side, were running full tilt down the hall. Then I lost consciousness.

Hours later I opened my eyes. The railings of the bed were raised and heavy blankets covered me. An IV dripped liquid into one arm and a blood-pressure cuff wrapped the other. A nurse looked down at me and smiled. Grogginess took over, and I slipped back into sleep. The next morning, as the nurse took my temperature and saw that I swallowed the pills she handed me, she said, "You had us worried yesterday. You went into anaphylactic shock, honey, probably a reaction to the dye."

I didn't know what she was talking about. The doctors never discussed what had happened, but there were no further attempts to X-ray my kidneys. Later, I learned about anaphylactic shock, and with that knowledge came belated fear and concern. My three children were under the age of five. There were no fantasies about a lovely death. The fear was not so much about my dying as it was about leaving my children. What would happen to them if I were to die now? It was easier to feel concern for my children than it was for me to address a potential reality of my death.

Another hospital experience followed surgery when the nurses and interns were in and out of my room in a flurry of activity for what seemed to be most of the night. Their concern was obvious to me, even in my semi-cognizant state. I was burning up with fever, frightened, and repeatedly feeling the sensation that I was drifting upward out of the left side of my body. Early in the morning, I was back in surgery. In the 1970s, patients were still being told little or nothing about the medical situation at hand. One nurse, however, whispered to me that she was praying for me, a bit of information that I found more disconcerting than comforting. Again, rather than acknowledge that I was mortal and my life transient, I worried that I did not have a will in place.

There were countless falls, beginning in childhood; falls from jungle gyms, out of trees, and from the bare backs of horses. The most serious fall, however, was when I fell backward into the stairwell and down a full flight of stairs. Fear gripped me as I felt myself in the air, for an instant touching nothing, and then hitting against walls, stair steps, and railings in a fall that seemed endless. Flailing arms tried unsuccessfully to grab on to something. My fall ended with my upper arm and shoulder striking the wrought-iron railings at the foot of the stairwell.

When my head cleared, my fear of falling was replaced by fear of how I would survive and support my kids. Newly divorced, self-employed, and raising three teenagers, I wondered how I would be able to work. Multiple injuries were complicated by the development of blood clots requiring a two-week stay in the hospital, followed by three months recuperation. Due to the extent of injuries, bones did not begin to mend for several weeks. Recuperation time was long and tedious. Residuals from that fall remain.

Over the years I have revisited that fall down the stairs an untold number of times, reflecting on its implications. What wisdom does that fall hold? What am I to learn? Why did I fall? Reflections yielded insights. For weeks before the fall I had mental images or dreams indicating that my life was going in the wrong direction. Some images were stark. I awoke from a dream just as my car travelling at high speed was going to hit a brick wall. Another dream, driving at night on a narrow, winding, unlit road, I swerved to miss a small furry animal and then realized that no animal was there. Was I going to run over and destroy something within me, something wild and vulnerable? Insights continued to arise over time. Long after my arm and hand regained most of their ability to function, I reinjured both arm and hand, although this time not seriously. However, it was serious enough to point out that relying on my right arm was not wise. My attitude had always been that when I needed a helping hand, I would find it at the end of my right arm. I confess now to the defiance imbued in my pseudo attitude of strength. Total self-sufficiency is a myth. Being responsible for myself is fine, but that does not preclude being open to help that comes from the depths of the unconscious as well as from the vast and sacred unknown.

The last time I played tag with death was in 1999. That time *knew that I was going to die.* On a sunny Sunday afternoon in December, exhausted and driving from Los Angeles to my home in Santa Barbara County, I dozed off at the wheel while driving about seventy miles an hour. As my tires hit the gravel between the freeway and the center divider, I woke up in a panic. Slamming on the brakes caused my car to spin out of control and into the speeding traffic. Everything moved in unreal, slow motion circles, and it was as though I were watching the entire scene. I waited in eerie calmness for the inevitable crash that I knew would kill me. Then the thought that I was going to die on the freeway hit me. On the freeway! No! Smashed flat by an 18-wheeler! Damn! Yet, I felt no fear. I was neither hit nor did I die. Instead, still moving in this delusory sense of slow motion, I observed casually as my car neared and crashed into the concrete overpass support, wiping out the passenger side of the car and turning the window into glass popcorn. A geyser spewed from the just-filled gas tank.

Sitting in the stopped car, I was amazed to find that I was not hurt. Slowly and methodically I tensed each muscle to check for the sharp pain of a broken bone, but no pain came. The words *I am not hurt, I am not hurt* echoed through my mind. A car pulled over on the far-side onramp. The driver talked on his cell phone. As I rolled down the window to signal him that I was all right, he frantically motioned me to stay where I was. I learned later that a woman had recently run onto the freeway after an accident, was hit by a car, and killed. He was obviously afraid I might do the same. Then it occurred to me to turn off the engine. I did and then rechecked my body, systematically flexing each muscle to reconfirm that nothing was broken. No sharp pains. I was fine and continued to reaffirm my good fortune, repeating softly to myself, "I'm not hurt. I'm not hurt. I'm all right." Two men pulled off the freeway ahead of me and ran back to my car to help. I thanked them and told them I wasn't hurt. When they asked if there was anything they could do, I realized I no longer had my glasses.

"Yes, can you please see if my glasses are any where?" They found them in the gravel several feet from the passenger side of the car, where they had flown through the now-non-existent glass in the window. The fire engine arrived. Next to arrive was a police car. The medics checked me out and took my blood pressure. It was its usual healthy number. I kept repeating that I wasn't hurt.

An ambulance was on the way. The police assumed I would take the ambulance to a hospital. "But I'm not hurt," I said. "I don't need an ambulance." No one seemed to be listening. The frustrated officer finally explained that he couldn't just leave me sitting on the ground by the freeway's center divider. I hadn't thought of that.

"I'll go with the tow-truck driver. My son can pick me up the junkyard, where they take my car."

He kept shaking his head as he told me I had to sign papers if I refused to go in the ambulance. I signed. The tow truck arrived. I walked over and asked the driver if I could ride with him and then climbed into the cab. He appeared a bit confused with the arrangement, but he was nice enough about it. The Highway Patrol officer got into his patrol car and drove off.

When my son Brad arrived to pick me up at the wrecking yard, he retrieved my things from my crumpled Toyota Camry and returned looking pale. I asked him to drive me home to Los Olivos. The thought of fixing myself some Miso soup and resting for a few days appealed to me.

"No, Mom. You're not going to like this, but I'm taking you home with me. Besides," he smiled, "you don't even have a car, so you don't get to choose."

Still somewhat dazed, I laughed. So much for dying on the freeway!

CHAPTER SEVEN

BEING WITH DEATH

In spite of my potentially ruinous encounter with the concrete overpass pillar, there were still times when I managed to do what most of us have managed to do, which was to fall back into my effective system of denial. Becoming conscious of one's denial is a convoluted process. I *get it*, and then *I lose it*. Death's presence continued to intrude. With the death of a very elderly and frail woman we knew, I was hit with the realization that I did not want to be trapped in this body forever, and that death could be a gift.

Gratitude entered the picture. The challenge is to integrate death as the final experience of life just as I have integrated the *Now* as the space in which I live my life. A greater connection with death arose, brought a brief wave of anxiety and then tranquility. My fear had given way to acceptance and gratitude, transmuting negative energies into creative energies of living that can grow only in places that are free of fear.

But what about the times when fear is our friend? Can comfort with death as a natural ending of life exist concurrently with the fear of death that protects us? I believe they can and do coexist. The healthy, protective, instinctive fear is the emotional state that provides stability, so that we don't consider jumping off a bridge whenever life gets a little sticky. It is a fear essential for our survival, the fear that demands we defend ourselves when we are attacked, or that we run from life-threatening danger. It is the *fight-or-flight* kind of fear. If a stranger were to break into my home, I would be terrified and do everything within my power to protect myself or escape. But if my doctor were to tell me that I had an incurable disease and probably had about three months to live, I trust that I would check over my paperwork to see that all the information was up to date and then prepare myself emotionally and spiritually to greet death with grace. I would spend time with family and friends, sharing my love for them and how much they mean to me.

With the exception of the periods of depression and contemplation of suicide as a young woman, I have devoted neither time nor energy to thoughts of voluntarily ending my life. My death fantasies were superficially dramatic and had no connection with the reality of actually dying. The consciousness, comfortable awareness, and acceptance of death that are with me today have come over time and are unlike either my former depression or my fantasies. One significant step came when I attended a lecture in the early 1970s given by a then-young doctor named Stanislav Grof and his then-wife Joan Halifax.[20] I listened transfixed as their lectures unfolded. First one would speak, and then the other, providing information and insights into how one might be present at another's death. Dr. Halifax told a gripping story of a young man who was dying and of the twists and turns and heart-stopping events that took place over his final few weeks of life. What struck me and stayed with me was the vitality of this young man's spirit. Here he was dying, and yet so alive. After being in a coma for about twenty-four hours, he awoke with total, clear, and accurate recall of what had transpired during that period of time he was not conscious. He commented to Dr. Halifax that she had changed her dress and gently chided her that she had cried a lot yesterday.

Less than a year after I attended that lecture, my mother died. Drawing from insights gained, I was able to be present with her in a meaningful way that would have been impossible before. During the final two weeks of her life, I was at her bedside. My teenage children took turns keeping vigil. My oldest son, sitting on the floor in the hall just outside the hospital room, fell asleep and for the rest of the night lay stretched out next to the wall. The nurses on the night shift covered him with a blanket and slipped a pillow under his sleeping head. Their patience in allowing him to spend the night there by his grandma's room brought me comfort. One nurse mentioned to me that she was touched to see his devotion to his grandmother.

Although my mother had weakened, she was alert and able to communicate. Over the following ten days I spent many hours sharing stories of childhood memories and reading her favorite poetry to her. I read those passages from the bible that she had so often read to me. For a short period of time, she would smile and sometimes say something. Other times she just smiled. Later she just lay there with her eyes closed. Certain that she could hear me, I continued telling her of things I remembered from my childhood. One of the treasured stories I shared was about the evening bath-time ritual she created for her three children. Each evening as Mama ran the bathtub full and before she was ready to plop us into warm water, she would take our dirty clothes, put them in the hamper, and then tell us to "Run, run, run! It's time to take your air baths." We raced around our small house in our bare bodies, squealing in delight. I'm sure it was after she had her fill of squealing that she caught us one by one. Then she would tell us what good children we were. She would lift an arm around to our backs so that the clavicle protruded and exclaim "Feel this! I do believe it is a wing about ready to sprout. You are such good children that you are about to sprout angel wings." Warm and glowing are my memories.

There were many stories. Mama grew up in the Willamette Valley in Oregon, which was known for its rain. Complaints about the weather were common, and my mother was determined that her children would learn to love the rain. Of course, we grew up in rain-starved Southern California, which made her job easier. Even so, she was incredibly successful. During the Great Depression, money was scarce, so her strategy for teaching the love of rain was simple. High on my parents' closet shelf sat a shoebox with the words *Rainy Day Toys* clearly marked. On a rainy morning we would be awakened with an excited whisper, "It's raining! Hurry and get up! We are having cinnamon toast and cocoa!" We would scurry out of beds. Cinnamon toast and cocoa were foods from Nirvana and our rainy-morning treat. I can remember shivering with excitement. My brothers and I danced around with glee when Mama brought the cinnamon toast. Immediately after breakfast, we followed Mama into the closest. As her three wide-eyed, eager children watched, she carefully removed the hallowed rainy-day toy box. We played with its treasures for hours. Later we indulged in another activity, which was reserved for and allowed exclusively on rainy days. We were allowed to turn over the chairs in the living room, drape throw rugs over them and make forts or hideouts. We would also take rain walks. Dressed in yellow slickers and rubber boots, we stopped often to listen to the raindrops on our rain hats. Mama would discuss just what kind of rain was falling, asking us "Was it baby rain? Children rain? Mama rain? Daddy rain?" We took our assignments very seriously as we made our designations as to just what kind of rain was falling. Home and dry, our last task of the day remained to be done. All of the forts must be dismantled, the rugs replaced, and chairs put upright before our father came home. The seriousness of putting things back in order somehow added to the adventure's secrecy and importance.

These and other stories were shared at bedside. Stories continued after she lost consciousness. I had learned that our ability to hear stays with us, even when in a coma. Although Mama did not respond, it was a comfort to feel that she could hear and was present. For almost two weeks the doctors said that they didn't understand how Mama held on to life. Finally, one doctor suggested that I give her permission to die. In my heart I wanted to scream "Don't die, Mama, please don't die." Instead, I whispered ever so softly, "It is all right for you to go. You do not have to stay here and suffer any longer. Mama, we love you so much. You're the most wonderful mama ever. Everybody will miss you, but that doesn't mean you have to stay and suffer. You are free to go to a place filled with peace and joy. Mama, you deserve peace and joy." She died within an hour.

As my grief slowly, slowly began to ease, the memory of my final days with the mother I loved so dearly brought added appreciation for what she had taught me during her lifetime and ultimately during the time she lay dying. The dignity of her death brought confidence that when my death comes, I will be able to be there, and like my mother, accept death with grace.

Most of us live with the loss of a loved one, a friend, or an acquaintance. Most have attended funerals or wakes or gatherings in remembrance. The older we are, the more people in our lives have been lost through death. My losses have been multiple and the accompanying emotions have ranged from somber respect, to a feeling of closure, to sadness, to devastating grief. Blessed with excellent health, my grandmother lived into her mid-nineties. She and my grandfather had celebrated their seventieth wedding anniversary a few years before she died. They raised five children and had a solid marriage. Money was scarce, and Grandma was a master at living frugally. When she fell and broke her hip, she worried and fussed about being taken to the hospital in an ambulance, complaining that it was far too expensive.

Shortly after returning home, she died in her sleep. My aunt, who was with her, said Grandma gave a sigh and was gone—a peaceful ending to a long, well-lived life. We would miss her, but no deep sadness surrounding her passing. It was time for her to go. Not all deaths are so peaceful. I have been with those in the grips of terror as well as with those who were at peace with dying. Just as our deaths are unique to who we are, so is our grieving the deaths of others. The loss of my son brought a depth of pain I did not know was possible. My mother's death tore me at the core of me. When my father died, I felt removed and relieved.

Exploration into the facets and dimensions of life and death continues. Perceptions of death change as do our perceptions of life. Once I laboriously waded hip deep through the demanding minutia of living. Now I experience *nothing-moments* that mean everything. James Hillman wrote, "First, soul refers to the deepening of events into experiences; (and) second the significance soul makes possible, whether in love or in religious concern, derives from its special relation with death."[21] The connection between life and death is one that current Western society finds difficult, but hope emerges. More voices speak out.

Throughout the ages, great minds have viewed death as the celebratory conclusion of life. Many cultures accept death as a natural part of life and see death as the ultimate transformative process. Common among Western attitudes is the tendency to see death as the ultimate test of modern medicine's prowess, a challenge, which modern medicine ultimately fails. However, Western attitudes are changing. One of the many things I have learned in the last several years is that we can continue to learn and grow until we breathe our last breath. During the final days and hours of life, radiance can emanate from the dying. I sat with an aged woman who glowed with a mystical beauty and serenity as she entered and moved through her process of dying.

Wisdom of others offers assurance. Thomas Edison's last words were when, just hours before his death, he woke from a coma and said "It is really beautiful over there." Steve Jobs' sister shared her brother's last words *"Oh wow! Oh wow! Oh wow!"* His words could well be interpreted as an ode to the beauty of death. Krishnamurti shares a truth we all know. "Everything on earth lives, dies, comes into being and withers away."[22] Jung describes death as a mysterious joining or union where the soul achieves wholeness.[23] The elegant and powerful words of Hafiz sum up the essence of death. "Wholeness, I think, draws its life somewhere where the breathing stops."[24]

CHAPTER EIGHT
THE ULTIMATE LOSS

Death has visited me often as it has visited many. My brothers died years ago. My closest friend since grade school who married my older brother died of cancer in her early sixties. Three of the five of us who hung out together since we were high school freshmen are now gone. Gone, too, are the cousins I grew up with, those who lived either nearby or with my family as siblings. My cousin June and I were the only girls in the extended family. Just a year apart, we were raised almost as sisters. She died three years ago. My forty-nine-year-old nephew died four years ago on Christmas, felled by a flu virus raging through Southern California.

Not all deaths can be looked upon as natural events. Disease is no respecter of age and cuts short the lives of infants, children, and adults alike. Violent, premature deaths rupture one's sense of how the natural processes of life should unfold. War takes lives indiscriminately, both the youth who fight the wars and the people who live in war zones. War is about fighting and dying, and our youth who make up the armies that do battle also make up the majority of those who die in battle. Although we know casualties will occur, deaths of young soldiers and civilians, including children, bring intense pain, even to those of us who do not know them.

Grieving and compassion are at times numbed as we are inundated with the death, the wounding, and the suffering rampant in the world today. As a child when I heard the stories of how the Romans made spectator sport of watching unarmed Christians fight hungry lions, I was horrified by the cruelty and sure that nothing like that could occur today. But it is as it always has been. The Romans did not have television and movies to bring slightly more palatable versions of the same fare, programs couched in the trappings of good fighting evil as wars are waged or murders solved. The Roman fascination with violence was direct and raw.

I remember a documentary about the Vietnam War where, in referring to the Vietnamese, a military officer explained that *those people don't really feel anything*. Immediately the camera moved to a Vietnamese family wailing inconsolably at a burial. Watching the film and listening to the pain of their voices was my first experience hearing people wailing. When I next heard wailing, it came up from the depths of me, from the sound of my own voice crying out and filling the room with my unbearable pain as I sat alone at night.

My oldest son was killed in a freak accident. The intensity of my grief seemed unbearable, yet we find the capacity to bear our grief. Grieving is deeply personal. It is our tribute to someone's meaning in our lives. It speaks to the permanence of death and shows up in sometimes simple ways—in the loneliness that comes with the realization that someone dear will never again drop by for coffee, will never share meaningful stories of life, fears, joys, defeats, and devastations, will never be there to share our pinnacles. Small things bring searing devastation. I was struck by despair when I first realized that I would never again answer the phone and hear him say "Hey, Mom." I wept when I heard that my twelve-year-old grandson kept calling his father's office to hear his voice on the answering machine.

The pain of losing someone to death comes with violent intensity. Losing a child brought remembrance of that moving documentary and with it an understanding that no one suffers alone. Shortly after Brad's death, a friend shared the words "To deny the grief is to diminish the gift." I did not deny my grief.

Life has taught me much, but it was Brad's death that taught me the dearness of life and profound acceptance of death. When Brad was killed, I didn't see how I could live, but I did live and in the process learned the immensity of my responsibility to live my life fully, to wring from each day the gifts of that day, some of which are not wrapped very nicely and are not seen as gifts at all when they arrive.

Brad, a building contractor, was instrumental in seeing that the home I was building as owner-builder made its way effectively and successfully through the construction process. His close friend Ed owned a large roofing company and donated a magnificent roof. The two of them came up once a year for a holiday of our own making called *Mama's House-Celebration Day.* They would bring good wine, and I would cook for days. They loved hors d'oeuvres, so hors d'oeuvres it always was. Each year I would make an array for brunch, more for an early afternoon indulgence, and another spread for late afternoon before they left to go back to Los Angeles. It was a great day, a floating holiday scheduled when both of them could break away from their hectic schedules.

It was February, 2003, and Brad and Ed were due in a week. Strangely, I could not bring myself to begin cooking, a ritual I had celebrated eagerly over the years. A friend was visiting, and I remember telling her that I felt strange, as though I were floating in eerie unreality, because I knew that Brad would not be coming. Twenty minutes later he called and told me that the engineers had made the necessary corrections to their drawings for the large construction project he was building. Brad was the contractor and needed to stay on-site with the crews. They would work over the weekend and put in long hours this coming week in order to get the project back on schedule.

"Can we move the day?" he asked.

"Sure," I said. "It's a floating holiday, remember?" My reluctance to start cooking and uneasiness about Brad's coming were now explained.

"Yeah. We'll have to float it this time. Ed is up to his eyebrows, too. Call him and see when we can reschedule. Tell him I'll need another week here."

We talked for a short time. I shared that I was feeling as though I might as well be pouring sand down a rat hole. I didn't feel that my efforts in helping resolve issues in our local school district were helping. Now an inappropriate and cruel policy was on the agenda. I was planning to present research that indicated how destructive the policy was for children but wondered if it were worth the time and effort.

"Mom, if you don't do it, nobody will."

That was on a Friday. Brad and I chatted for a few more moments and said goodbye. It was the last time I heard his voice.

On Saturday, for some reason, I decided to clean the garage. My phone on the nightstand was not working, so I was relieved to find another old phone that I had stored in the garage cabinet and forgotten. It was an old-fashioned clunker with the spiral plastic cord connecting the receiver to phone. I immediately plugged it in beside my bed. The first time it rang was Saturday night around midnight, waking me from a sound sleep. The call was my friend Faith asking me if she could come by. Of course, she could come by. My first thought was that something had happened, and she needed to see me.

"Where are you?" I asked.

"In your driveway," she said.

A fire in the woodstove had been prepared for morning. I quickly lit it and opened the front door. My son Derek had called Faith and asked her please to go and be with me. He didn't want me to be alone when I received the call that Brad had been killed.

The death of my son was violent, premature, and unexpected. He was forty-nine when he was killed in a freak accident on the construction site. He left a wife and two sons. He left a brother, sister, and mother. He left nieces and nephews, aunts and uncles. He left cousins and friends. He left the guys he worked with. He left people who loved him.

Brad's service was bathed in an air of unreality. I sat mute. Words of Shakespeare kept playing in my mind. "All the world's a stage." Life is a stage, and on the stage where Brad played out his life, the curtain had fallen too soon. We all should rise in standing ovation to honor him. Our applause would roar and reach the heavens where Brad was surfing the winds, and he would stop, for he would hear us, and he would know how deeply he touched our lives and how much we loved him.

But that is not what happened. The minister, who was a relative, rambled on about Brad, a man he hardly knew. The mayor spoke. As a gaggle of hungry pigeons masquerading as doves were released from their cages to fly home for dinner, people wept. The service was over. Grieving, people silent and somber, walked away slowly. Having no comprehension that pain of such depth existed, I stood immobilized.

A year had passed since Brad's death, and on that rainy February morning I was sitting in my usual chair, embracing the warmth of the early morning fire in the wood stove, having my first cup of coffee, and realizing that my life needed attention. It was time to pull things together, to put my life in order. It was time for healing. The rain picked up its intensity, its pounding filling the room with hypnotic sound and wrapping me in deep meditation.

A dream came to me, but I was not asleep. In fact, I was quite conscious as I sat there in my living room. It was as though I were watching a video in color. It was like a different kind of dream. I had heard of waking dreams. Was this one? It seemed so normal and appropriate. In this dream I was the focus of a ceremony. In it, all kinds of beings were preparing me to be born into my earth life. There I stood, my full adult self. It was crazy but perfectly logical in the dream. There was much bustling and busy-ness with angels, saints, and guides everywhere, an obviously important event. I stood in the dream, surrounded by adult beings, all of them making a big fuss over me. There were flowing diaphanous blue fabrics and large jugs, the kind featured in Sunday school books. An enthusiastic plumpish, woman was telling me that I would have three children who would bring me great joy. Then a man's voice, clear and unemotional, interrupted the gaiety.

"Your middle child, your oldest son, will be killed in an accident. The pain will be unfathomable for you." He paused for an imperceptibly brief moment and then asked, *"Would you rather not have this child?"*

It was as though the man were making sure everything was in order for my imminent birth, as though he had a punch list of some sort. I jolted alert. The room still held the feelings of the dream. Hesitant to speak aloud, I pleaded in a whisper of desperation.

"I must have this child! I will take the pain of the universe. Just give me this child. I must have this child! I want this child."

Hearing myself, I quieted. Sitting very still, I said softly to myself, *"Lois, you were given this child. You had this child. Your pain is irrelevant."*

I miss him beyond measure and will always miss him, yet my mourning had shifted. When times come bringing a deluge of pain washing over and through me, the joy of him prevails. The greatest part of me lives in gratitude that he was born to me, that for forth-nine years he was my son here in our physical world, and that we were very close. Death had reached into my innermost precious life. It could reach anywhere. Although knowing life is temporary and accepting that death is permanent and awaits us all, never has death brought greater anguish than when it took my son.

With time, life regained its normalcy. Anticipation returned. I again made lists of things to be done or activities on tap for the coming day. I dared to plan ahead. Now, as I turned attention to the revitalization of my life, more thought was given to life's precarious nature. Death had now taken up permanent residence in my consciousness. I knew death was making its inexorable way toward me, framing my life within the bookends of a life span. When my mother died, I remember thinking that she had completed her life, that her time on earth had come and was now gone. When I thought in those finite terms, I found myself stunned and surprised to realize that my mother's life was over. Now my son had completed his life. It was too early for him to die. Suddenly, the span of one's lifetime seemed incredibly brief.

Each year, on Brad's birthday, on Christmas, and on the anniversary of his death, I light a candle and give my thoughts to him. Nine years after his death, on February 21, 2012, I lit a candle by his picture, smiled at him, and told him again how much I miss him. On this ninth anniversary of his death, something was different. It took awhile for me to realize that the difference was that my grief had healed.

How could this be? How did this happen? How will I ever explain this shift in how my mourning had become memory? I still love him so, and miss him so, and rejoice in the gift of his life. Will some think me callous that I no longer mourn? Filled with a sense of being vulnerable, of being judged as an unworthy mother if I no longer grieved, I understood immediately how one could hold on to grief in tribute to someone so cherished or hold on to grief as one holds a loved one close. I also understood for the first time that healing is possible, and that I had somehow been given the permission to heal. Peace filled me. Brad would be pleased.

The demands to live my life with awareness and in gratitude were never clearer. It was my job and responsibility to do so. Now old, more relaxed, and philosophical, I choose to believe that we die when our time comes to die. Since I have no evidence one way or the other, this belief continues to bring comfort. In the time between now and whenever death comes for me, I want to honor the gift of my life, including those final days and hours. Brad would have wanted no less of me.

CHAPTER NINE

THE PURPOSE OF PAIN

In a world that expects us to stay young, thin, and happy, admitting fear and pain can be an up-hill battle, especially our fear of death. No one stays young any longer than the years allocated to youth. Many stay healthy and vibrant far beyond those youthful years, but that is not the same as staying young. While no one can stop the clock, a few do succeed in staying thin as years advance. Happiness is another story. It is wonderful. Bask in it when it comes, but realize that happiness comes and goes. The ubiquitous, bright yellow circle, that flat, shiny paper sticker with an expressionless fixed smile is an appropriate symbol for a perpetually unreal and superficial state that remains out of reach.

Happiness is one of the multiple emotions we experience as we move into and out of varying situations in our daily lives. Different emotions are called up in response to dissimilar experiences. Feeling joy, sadness, satisfaction, discouragement, envy, fear, caution, enthusiasm, love, dislike, confidence, insecurity, skepticism, hatred, compassion, anger, and anxiety is to feel emotion. Feeling fear, anger, anxiety, or sadness can overwhelm other emotions. They tell us that we are not happy, and society tells us that if we are not happy, something is wrong with us. Advertisements ask: "Are you happy?" If not, call this number. There is medicine for you. Taking a pill to induce a palatable emotional state, whether or not it is appropriate, cuts us off from feeling an array of emotions. When happiness is inappropriate, we do not understand the message carried in the pain of sadness. It is important to realize that natural happiness is not a fixed state of being. Breathing is a fixed state of being. The heartbeat is a fixed state. If either condition falters, see a doctor.

There are times when medication to relieve extreme unhappiness or depression is necessary. Many times, however, we have the unrealistic belief that appropriate sadness or unhappiness is not normal. When something sad happens, it is not the time to feel happy. It is the time to feel sad. When sadness or unhappiness is unrelenting, one must look within for ways to change the circumstances triggering that unhappiness. Seeking counseling from a therapist might be helpful in finding ways to resolve unrelenting painful emotions. Buying into what is unrealistic or impossible creates a new set of anxieties. We disguise our worry about dying beneath our fear of getting old or gaining weight; we worry ourselves sick because we are not always happy. Is worrying all the time about not being happy less frightening than worrying all the time about death? Who knows? What is important is that we realize we do not have to spend our lives worrying.

Our desire for consistent happiness removes our ability to address our pain and its possible source or probable message. When pain reaches into our emotional core, its impact is huge. If pain is so common, it must have a purpose. And what is that purpose? What is our pain telling us? What factors in our lives are the sources of our pain? Inducing an artificial state of happiness prohibits us from understanding and learning from pain. Whether it is physical or emotional, it is there to protect us. First, it gets our attention. It tells us something is wrong. Physical pain is easier to understand and respond to than emotional pain, which Dr. Michael Kearney calls *soul pain*, "the pain that fills us with deep sadness, immobilizes us, and blocks our way to recognizing and feeling joy."[25]

The ever-sought-after, nonexistent, around-the-clock version of happiness remains our elusive goal, yet happiness is not something we can find *out there*. Eleanor Roosevelt (1884- 1963) once wisely said that Happiness is not a goal; it is a by-product. Instead of happiness, think of an inner sense of contentment, a feeling of peace that comes with a deep and underlying satisfaction with being the person you are. Appreciate the value system you live by, and how you deal with the everyday comings-and-goings of life. Accept your foibles. Being at peace with who you are serves as the base from which to navigate the emotional challenges of life. I envision contentment as the keel on the sailing ship that goes deep into the waters of life, keeping the vessel of my being from capsizing, holding it steady through the rough, stormy seas of life and into the calm waters that follow. Contentment also makes possible the capacity to move with reasonable comfort through not only the ups-and-downs of life but also the ever-present days of ordinariness. It provides the foundation from which one can experience the intense challenges of fear, rage, helplessness, and grief and not be washed away by those emotional storms. It provides a foundation on which to build our capacity for joy, the happiness of sharing time with friends and family, working at a job that is challenging and rewarding, buying a coveted item, watching the magic of a sunrise or a rainbow—simple experiences that can add further meaning to our lives.

Contentment nurtures our capacity to have loving relationships with people who are not perfect, just as we are not perfect. Storms do not last forever, and the calm waters that follow rough seas can bring deep appreciation for the smoother times. As a culture we seek happiness and try at all costs to avoid pain. We seek meaning and fill the void with things. We confuse good parenting with raising perpetually happy children and ply them with things to assure that they do not suffer deprivation. In doing so, we deny our children their connection with reality. We skim the shallows, daring not to dive deeply into life's complexity.

The alchemists were on to something. Working with forge and crucible, they knew that both transformation and crisis contained the Sacred. It is within the cauldron of pain where new insights arise. As we live life, let us embrace pain as well as ecstasy, fear along with fearlessness, and view all as our teachers. As we move forward with our arms filled with the abundance of living, we continue to find ourselves strangely empty handed. Answers are again not clear. What we were sure we understood is now confusing to us. Clearly, life's road is neither level nor is it a smooth and steady line. During those uneven times are opportunities for trusting as we learn from life's pain.

They are also times for sorting out and letting go, so that priorities can fall into place. Through all of this comes a greater philosophical perspective on death.

With age, one accepts that pain is an integral part of life. If it is true that for everything there is a time, then there is a time for pain. Who among us has not felt the world closing in? Has anyone not known the urge to strike out or take flight? When carefully constructed walls crumble, who has not wanted to cower and hide but could not? Sometimes it is important to know that there is a time for crying, a time for allowing the pain into every cell of the body, for breathing it in. Only by embracing pain, by finding its hidden value, can we let the pain go. Then we can begin to heal. We can accept what is and go on. Move through pain, not around it. Do not stay in your pain and wallow, basking in the pseudo solace of victimhood. Pain is important. It builds the muscles of our souls. It teaches that out of our vulnerability we can become stronger.

Our lives begin amid pains of childbirth. Throughout life we address pains of living. Finally, we know the pains of death. Most often physical pain is accompanied by emotional pain, although either is capable of standing alone. Both physical and emotional pain exists in all lives. When pain is interpreted as meaningless and unjust, it feeds self-pity. Seeking understanding and finding resolution allows one to move through the pain and beyond it. One walks into and through the metaphorical fires of life, feels the heat and suffers the burns, and comes out stronger. Walking around the fires of pain does not allow for healing. If we are diligent and have courage, we resolve the messages pain brings, which in turn frees us to walk on and into our lives. When we have done so we are changed. We are stronger and wiser. The question is no longer "Why me?" The question becomes "What does this teach me, and do I learn its lesson?"

Pain is our teacher, especially soul pain, "which is the experience of an individual who has become disconnected and alienated from the deepest and most fundamental aspects of himself or herself,"[26] pain that is beyond the pain of the ego. It is ever the catalyst, pushing us into places we are often loath to go. The practical side of me demands involvement of the intellect. I want to figure this out. But it is intuition that taps the psyche, the soul, where in some unknown, unseen way it has been kept apprised of what lies in the vast, seminal morass of the unconscious. Bits of information come forth when the time is right. What is unknown to us is how the psyche is kept posted, guiding us, surrounding us with experiences rife with wisdom that we can gather into ourselves as the building blocks of our wholeness.

Although pain is not pathology, medications developed to ameliorate the emotional pain of depression are among the most popular drugs on the market. There are times when these medications are necessary. Other times they are not. The pressure on all of us to be happy all the time has resulted in a society sustained on mood-altering medication. Attempting to avoid all emotional pain can render us incapable of feeling joy. To engage our pain, we must have the courage to feel, to open the doors to the forbidden, which in light of our all-consuming search for happiness, can be daunting and at times terrifying.

Writers, philosophers, and poets have brought clarity to the honored role of pain. Some of my favorite words were written by Alexander Lowen and paraphrased by Phillip Slater in his book *Earthwalk*.

> Without despair we cannot cast our
> allegiance to reality. It is a kind of
> mourning period for our fantasies . . .
> [yet] no real growth within a person
> can occur without it.[27]

According to Lowen, the role of despair, which is commonly perceived as the villain in people's lives, holds an all-important place in our pursuit of happiness. He tells us what we prefer not to hear, that "The path to joy leads through despair."[28] Carl Jung wrote extensively on the power of suffering, saying that "A man who has not passed through the inferno of his passions has never overcome them."[29] He also told the world "There is no coming to consciousness without pain."[30] Pain serves as a catalyst for personal transformation when one is open to the possibilities of first embracing the pain followed by understanding the wisdom that pain holds out to us. Kahil Gibran is asked to tell us of pain.

> Your pain is the breaking of the shell that
> encloses your understanding.
> Even as the stone of the fruit must break,
> that its heart may stand in the sun,
> so must you know pain.[31]

Once understood, pain can dissipate, and one can move on to a more expansive level of consciousness. Pain and suffering of our hearts and souls, when met honestly and embraced in spite of our suffering, when we allow ourselves to *feel it through*, we can pick its bones for meaning. Then we can let it go and begin to develop the courage, strength, and confidence that allow joy to come in.

Parents can wisely screen and translate pain, thus allowing their children to learn and grow from their exposure to pain that is an integral and unavoidable component of life. Trying to shelter children from all pain is not possible. Pain finds its way to us. It is intrinsic to life. Being denied an acceptance of pain as part of life can create an impenetrable barrier to finding a realistic acceptance that life at times hurts. Extremely sheltered lives offer the temptation to remain shallow.

I know what it is to be haunted by depression. Death would call out to me, offering comfort and release. There are those of us who cried out in our pain and asked, as Pushkin asked "Life, why wert thy given me?"[32] A.E. Housman struck a chord with me when I was in the throes of youth's turmoil. I was seventeen when introduced to Housman and read his poetry over and again as he poured out his dark and cynical obsession with injustice and death. My favorite speaks from the grave for English soldiers killed in war.

> Here dead we lie
> Because we did not choose
> To live and shame the land
> From which we sprung.
> Life, to be sure,
> Is nothing much to lose
> But young men think it is
> And we were young.[33]

Reading the work of poets who grappled with death began years ago when I was wrestling with my own unknown demons of death. Hafiz and Rumi have taken the places of Housman, Swinburne, Pushkin, and others. I now can resonate with Tennyson's confident acceptance of death in this stanza from his poem, *Crossing the Bar:*

> Sunset and evening star
> And one clear call for me!
> And be there no moaning at the bar,
> When I put out to sea.[34]

My dalliance with Dylan Thomas' defiance of death "Do not go gentle into that good night"[35] has softened. I am no longer young, and when it is my time, I feel confident that I can go *gentle* and in peace into that *good night*. But we shall see.

Age can bring warmth and mellowness and an acceptance of human vulnerability and mortality. Often the pervasive, vague fear of everything and nothing dissolves when it becomes clear that the fear lurking just out of reach is the fear of death. Old age holds the possibility of walking with death and of understanding and accepting the role of pain in the process of transformation. Today, I am at peace as I walk with Thanatos over these final miles, able to enjoy the scenery and abundance of life.

CHAPTER TEN

HOSPICE AND PALLIATIVE CARE

Volunteering with hospice beckoned to me, and since the doctoral program required a summer project, hospice felt right, yet the reasons compelling me had not gelled. Once started, I realized that the seeds had been planted years before, when my ninety-three-year-old aunt was dying, and being with her made me feel inadequate and uncomfortable. I did not know what to say or do and would leave without saying a word and feeling ashamed. Now, while my logical self wondered why I was drawn to sit at the bedside of a dying stranger, a deep knowing within me knew that I had made the right decision.

Had I not known enough of death? Would the experience of being with dying strangers bring me greater understanding? Would it allow me to be there and express compassion without the intense pain of grieving the loss of someone dear to me? What if being there in the face of death brought forth my overpowering need to make things better—those leftover little-girl feelings of wanting to please? End-of-life care is for those who will not get well. They will not even get better. There is no cure for dying. At hospice, curing is not the goal. In our fix-it culture, my need to fix things has found numerous avenues for expression. At hospice there would be nothing for me to fix.

Acceptance. I would learn acceptance, and in doing so would care for and tend to, comfort and listen. I would be present in death's presence, freeing myself to be truly present in my own life. What actually took place was profound. Conversations unlike any I had ever known would weave webs of connections and closeness, allowing deep and intimate sharing. Being present with the dying, I learned to recognize and own my reconciliation with the air, the aura, or the atmosphere unique to death.

While being introduced to palliative care and surrounded by like-minded people, I found that I was not alone in my desire to be conscious and present at my death. Both volunteers and professional staff validated the feelings that had been with me for decades. A natural and reasonably comfortable death, even in cases of severe illness, was both desirable and possible. I felt a gentle exhilaration when people at hospice confirmed the idea of death as a profound and sacred transformational experience. I felt validated, not in the ego sense of being right, but in a sense of deep belonging to the rhythms of life and death. The possibility of being free of the fear of dying was real.

Reading books on death brought a deluge of information on the subject. Attitudes are shifting in how society addresses the role of death in our lives. Acceptance of palliative care as loving and humane is rapidly on the rise. The intense, multifaceted emotions surrounding death are finding their ways into our conversations. Articles, television shows, books, and documentaries are increasingly writing about end-of-life issues. The subject of death is making its way into mainstream consciousness. We are almost able to accept, anticipate, and talk about death's presence, about the aspects we must address, and about the plans that need to be in place. Death might one day be a topic of conversation over coffee or perhaps the subject of talk over wine and cheese after all.

Throughout history many cultures have accepted death as life's natural ending, a time for giving comfort and a time of honoring completion of life's journey—the basic tenet on which hospice was originally founded. With the advance of Western medicine, attitudes shifted. New and improved ways to cure illness became and continue to be available. Miraculous machines and miracle medicines began saving lives and continue to do so. Death became the adversary. Often it is the adversary and is defeated, at least in the immediate crisis. Some treatments and medications, however, are invasive and painful, and cause unnecessary suffering. When recovery is possible or probable, the prospect of overcoming disease is worth the suffering. When no chance of recovery exists, many are asking why such harsh treatments are administered. For the elderly or terminally ill, why are we so determined to do everything we can do to wring out a bit more time for a few more breaths before death takes over? Why do people feel so obligated to stop death when it is death's time to come? Why inflict agony when recovery is not possible? Why use harsh treatment when it takes from a person the possibility of a more tranquil death?

The reasons are multiple. Is it because we ourselves are afraid of death? Do we need to feel that everything possible was done to save the life of someone we love? Or is it someone we don't love—unloved ones die, too—and are we afraid that we will be judged or condemned if we fail to order every treatment possible? If we just let a loved one die, will we be haunted by guilt?

Dame Cicely Saunders, nurse, social worker, and physician, witnessed dying patients being either ignored or subjected to painful, useless procedures when there was no chance of getting well and recognized a need for a different kind of care. She founded hospice as an alternative to hospital care for those who were terminally ill, and in 1969, opened the doors at St. Christopher's Hospice in South London, England. Acting on her belief that the way care is given can reach into the most hidden places,[36] she dedicated her life to the premise that a person's life holds value for as long as that person lives. Her compassion empowered others to be with the dying, to embrace death as the natural ending of life, and to offer comfort, understanding, and meaning to one's final days. She introduced ways to address relationship completion by saying to the dying the healing words "I forgive you, forgive me; I love you, and good-bye."[37] She insisted that, as the significance of each life is honored, so must the significance of each death be honored.

In reality, few spend time thinking about how we will honor the significance of our lives as we are dying.

Instead, we spend our time thinking about a much more pleasant subject: staying young and, of course, keeping our youthful beauty intact. We nurture the fantasy that perfection can be ours. In our fantasy-perfect worlds, we do not die; in the real world, we do die. When the time comes when cure is not possible, there are few medical paradigms to resolve or even address the situation. In today's world, the inability to fix what is wrong can leave one feeling helpless, especially when faced with the death of someone to whom we are deeply attached. In our crowded and costly medical institutions, there is rarely a place for a patient who will not get well to find serenity in simply being comforted while dying. When the body can no longer heal, it is the soul that needs attention. Palliative care can ease the physical pain, allowing for the healing of the soul.

A former English professor who wanted to become a nurse, Teresa Brown, RN,[38] writes a gripping account of her first year in the oncology ward of a major U.S. hospital. She tells of curing and failing to cure, of demands bordering on the impossible, and of the sometimes caring and other times barbaric practices that currently exist in our medical institutions. Current laws or hospital policies often state that, unless one has directed the hospital in writing do not resuscitate, numerous procedures, many of which are painful and frightening, will be administered. We all know that there are many times when a person's life can and should be saved and where Code Blue is essential. In the context of this book, Code Blue is discussed when being ordered for a person who is in the process of dying and when death is imminent, and when ordering invasive procedures leaves the patient with no possibility of having a calm, comfortable, or peaceful death that might have been available in another setting. In the throes of Code Blue, one has neither time nor presence of mind to say good-bye to loved ones.

Offering palliative care to those dying at home or in hospice facilities is in stark contrast to the medical modes practiced in the majority of hospitals. Hospice creates an atmosphere of inclusiveness, opening the way for those of us left to grieve to reach acceptance and find a degree of peace. The overriding spirit of palliative care includes the profound honoring of every stage of life, including acceptance of the inevitability of death and the experience of dying. Tending the dying includes comforting, listening, and responding. There are also times to just sit quietly at bedside.

Death is the real thing, as is life. It is a complex transcendence that exists in contradiction to our dread and denial. According to Jung, when one feels that a death is appropriate, it can be seen as a returning home, a haven for the soul, and a welcoming into the arms of a Sacred Deity. But when death is violent, premature, unjust, or preventable, it can be perceived as a theft, as a brutal stealing away of someone dear, where grief can be complicated by rage at the injustice of it all.

As we seek resolution with death, the work done by Megory Anderson,[39] as described in her beautiful book *Sacred Dying*, provides simple, meaningful ways to honor and give solace to the dying. She is a leading example of an emerging profession made up of people trained to assist not only the dying but also those who live and grieve. The impact of her writing as she shares the profound experiences of her connections with the dying at a soul level is powerful and comforting. Reading her book moved me more deeply into feelings of being at ease with death. Death was becoming less and less of a stranger.

CHAPTER ELEVEN

CHARLES AND ALICIA

While we associate death with pain, suffering, and loss, life itself holds its share of the same. With birth, a new life joins us. With death, we lose someone. Our pain is wrapped in our feelings of loss and separation. We desperately miss someone's presence in our lives. A vast empty space deep within us aches. We associate pain with death. Pain also accompanies birth, yet rarely if ever would someone greet a birth announcement by wincing at the memory of hard labor. Even when death is peaceful, painless, and timely, we weep our tears of loss. Another of today's trends is to deny mourning and in lieu of suffering and sadness, we are to celebrate the life of the deceased. It sounds lovely, but celebration must wait. Our pain is too raw. It must be attended to. Attempting to celebrate too soon denies the grief we feel and the searing pain of mourning that is inherent in the healing process. In today's culture, the mantra is: *Don't cry. Celebrate. Be happy.* Yet as we attend these services of celebration, pain comes forth, sometimes uncontrollably. Perhaps the soul knows better and insists that we honor our mourning before moving on to a celebration. Then, we can begin to heal.

There are times when death does not bring mourning, but instead, a profound sense of the spiritual power of the Sacred. Two deaths of people I knew briefly brought home to me the sacredness of death. Both moved me deeply. I was visiting Sarah House, an eight-bedroom home for end-of-life care in Santa Barbara, California. Sarah House offers a social–model hospice, where residents share a home and live together as members of a family. I was meeting with the director, Dr. Stephen Jones, when he was called to tend to a resident. Before leaving he asked me to sit with Charles for a short time until he returned. Entering Charles' room, we saw him lying motionless, his eyes open and staring blankly. Dr. Jones signaled me to sit in the chair next to Charles' bed and then bent down beside me, making introductions.

"Charles, this is my friend, Lois. She's come to be with you for a while. She is a loving person, an angel."

"Hello, Charles." My voice was almost inaudible.

Dr. Jones turned to me. Speaking clearly and comfortably, as though we were meeting at a social function and as though Charles were alert and able to participate, he told me about Charles, his family, and his service during WWII. Charles had led a combat team of soldiers who fought in the deep snows of the Alps. The soldiers were on skis and carried heavy backpacks. Charles' team suffered heavy losses, although fewer than were lost in other ski teams. He had been awarded a medal for his valor.

Before leaving the room, Dr. Jones commented that the rails on Charles' bed were up because Charles kept moving over to the side of the bed. "He's making sure there is room for his wife Mary. We don't want him to fall."

For not more than fifteen or twenty minutes I sat at Charles' bedside as he lay dying. When I touched his hand he did not respond. An overwhelming sense came to me that Charles was deep within himself in a place, where he was doing the work of dying. I could sense his total focus. There was no forceful intensity of energy, just a soft, all-encompassing focus in a space that held nothing but space. Occasionally, he twitched as though he were separating the soul bit-by-bit from the physical body. He stared peacefully at something I could neither see nor imagine. Initially, it seemed that I should be doing something, but I released that feeling. The only thing to be doing was to be respectfully present, humbled to be allowed at his bedside, honoring this sacred time. With each jerking movement, was he freeing another soul-body connection necessary to complete the transition of his death? It seemed so to me.

Charles died early the next morning. Those few minutes with a dying man, a stranger, opened a vision of dying that I had neither contemplated nor experienced. Why should dying not be an intense experience that demands total focus and concentrated effort, just as birthing a new life takes total focus and concentrated effort? Being allowed to be present and briefly share a most sacred time impacted me profoundly. Charles will live forever in my memory.

During my work as a hospice volunteer, I met with a woman twice and sometimes three times a week during the last month of her life. Her name was Alicia. Pancreatic cancer had ravaged her body, and she was in the final stages of the disease. Although Alicia was as frail as a whisper, her beauty could not be hidden. When I mentioned to her that she was a beautiful woman, she smiled and pointed to a photo on the dresser of herself as a young woman. Indeed, she was a rare beauty, but now in her death, her beauty was enhanced by a glow, a soft radiance. I had read of the phenomenon when a dying person was wrapped in a radiant glow. To witness this shining through of the soul was a privilege.

When I first came, Alicia was alert and wanted to talk. Her thoughts were consumed with the things she would do once she was well. She was looking forward to being with her new grandchild due to be born in three months. Alicia had one daughter and a granddaughter with whom she was close and with whom she wanted to spend more time. One afternoon after sharing her plans of what she would do when she got well, she was silent for a while and then said softly, "If I get well." The direction of our conversations shifted. She now shared things she had done of which she was particularly proud. Early life was difficult and lonely. Raised by a single mother who worked in the fields of the San Joaquin Valley, Alicia spent much of her time alone, fantasizing playmates and making up games. It was clear that she was an intelligent and creative child who grew up to be an intelligent and gracious woman.

Conversations shifted again. Alicia worried that her life had not counted, and she wanted to know that her life did count. She wanted to feel reassured that she had lived in a helpful way. She wanted to know that God would approve. Fear of her failure to have pleased God gnawed at her. She had single-handedly raised her daughter and worried that because she had been financially stretched to meet the basic costs of getting by, she had not given her daughter many of the material things that other children enjoyed. I assured her that she had given her daughter the most important things there are to give. She had given her daughter love, guidance and encouragement.

"Alicia, I've met your daughter. She's a lovely and loving mother. I see her with her daughter, patient and kind. She loves you deeply. You gave her perfect gifts. Kids don't need stuff. They need mamas who love and guide them. You have done that."

Alicia enjoyed listening to poetry, and I read my favorites to her. I read her favorite passages from her Bible, its margins neatly noted with her precisely written comments. While reading from her Bible, and in mock surprise, I would pause and tell her,

"Alicia, I don't find anywhere in the Bible where God demands of us or even tells that we are to buy a bunch of stuff for our kids. It appears that you have done exactly what God wanted you to do. God asks that we love one another. You are a loving soul. He asks that we be kind and that we live honestly, and that we do our work well. You have done all of that. God asks us to love our children and teach them values to live by and give our child the knowledge that she is loved. Alicia, you have done everything you needed to do. I am sure that God is very proud of you and lovingly waits for you to come home."

It had become almost banter between us, she wanting to know that she had pleased God, and I telling her the many ways in which she had. One afternoon as we talked, Alicia smiled. In a murmur so soft I strained to hear her, she whispered,

"You validate me."

"Ah, you use the perfect word: *validate*! Only something true can be validated. You know that. You were a bookkeeper for an accountant. You validated the numbers. Now you know that deep inside yourself lies the truth. The love, beauty, kindness, and compassion within you tell how you lived your life. Yes, Alicia, you are validated!"

She lay in bed, paper thin and fragile and smiled. "You got me," she whispered and smiled again. Soon it was time for me to leave. "See you Friday," I said softly.

She whispered back, "See you Friday."

Alicia died on Friday, minutes before I arrived. I stood by her bedside and almost inaudibly breathed words, trusting that she might hear me from the other side, thanking her for coming into my life, for showing me what it truly is to die gracefully.

Defying time, this friendship forged itself into being. The indelible, delicate impressions she made on me will be with me for my lifetime. My connection with Alicia was profound. I remember her with deep love, but I do not confuse those feelings with grief. Losing my son brought paralyzing grief. Alicia brought me the gift of knowing her, of spending sacred and intimate time with her as she moved through the final stages of her life and into and through her death.

Once home, I lit a candle, read aloud a poem she loved, and wept silently, but not in mourning. I wept because the depth of my feelings found no other way to honor our brief, intense, and poignant bond. For this powerful gift of human connection and feeling the humble privilege of being with her during her last days, I wept, moved by the immensity of it all.

CHAPTER TWELVE

RITES, RITUALS, AND CEREMONIES

What we know and what believe are often defined and structured in rites, rituals, and ceremonies, the majority of which are endowed with spiritual significance. As with most human endeavors, whether in the creation of our ceremonies or in the everyday structure of our lives, we have a tendency to reify the Sacred and deify the mundane. Attitudes and beliefs can shift over time and impact our ceremonial traditions while still helping us keep order in ours lives, bring us joy and gratitude, as well as help us overcome fear.

Among cultures and customs, religions and traditions, one finds many variations in how people honor events. Some differ widely; others share much in common. All honor their deceased. Most beliefs offer a safe structure for expressing anguish and a setting for honoring the dead and mourning their loss. In others, while not suppressed, excessive and prolonged mourning is discouraged and a joyous release of the soul encouraged. Some groups require or accept cremation; others prohibit it. The examples given here represent a cursory look at aspects of a few traditions relating to death. Their purpose is to offer a glimpse into the range of ways humankind pays tribute to those who have died while offering acceptable ways to express grief.

Celtic customs, as with many others, include holding a wake during which the body of the deceased is displayed in an open casket so mourners can pay tribute to the loved one and grieve his departure. Burial is not rushed. Before taking leave, the soul needs time to say good-bye to the body that must stay on earth and thank it for being the soul's home while here.

In the Jewish tradition burial takes place as soon as possible after death, preferably the next day. Traditional and Reform Jews share versions of the same traditions but differ in detail. The deceased is buried in a simple pine coffin, thus removing all reference to status in life. Typically, there are no flowers. At graveside, mourners place a few handfuls of dirt over the coffin symbolizing a gift that was neither requested nor can be reciprocated. Shiva, a seven-day period of mourning, follows the burial. Cremation is not allowed.

Shamanic death rituals consist of recapitulation, forgiveness, and granting permission to die. The purpose of death rites is to assist the dying in experiencing a peaceful death. Shamanic rites often include a group of family or tribal members who aid in facilitating death, participating in rituals to help the Light Body or Luminous Field[40] disengage. Finally, they clear and close the chakras so the soul will find its way to The Sacred Universe and not reenter the body.[41]

Traditions in Hindu death rituals are based on the Vedas and are quite consistent, containing few variations throughout the different castes, sects, and regions. Most deaths take place at home and men conduct all rituals. As death nears, family is notified and gathers to keep vigil. Detailed rituals are followed before and after death. When the body is cremated, the ashes are placed in the Ganges River or in other rivers. If there is no river near, the ashes and bones are buried. Lengthy mourning is discouraged.

Western culture encompasses multiple religions with varying customs that are not covered here. There are, however, common practices worthy of note. In many hospitals, policies unrelated to religious affiliation require that two hours after death, the body of the deceased is classified as a cadaver and must be removed. A hospice setting holds a different atmosphere. Free from restricting policies, a grieving family will find support in a more relaxed and supportive setting. Hospice care is available to those who opt to die at home with families, and where the potential for a peaceful death is greater.

People tend to find comfort in staying with what is familiar. One's belief system, be it a cultural custom or a religious belief, can offer the comfort and safety needed in times of crisis or vulnerability. When our personal and family beliefs collide, the impact on this more intimate level can be stressful. The collision of cultures that take place within families as well as communities can result in poignant emotional fallout. Lucia,[42] the daughter of an Anglo mother from an educated middle-class family and a Hispaño father from Northern New Mexico, grew up Coyote, someone born to parents of different ancestries. In spite of being raised under her Anglo mother's tutelage, Lucia identified with her father's Hispanic community.

The ways in which these two cultures honored and approached death were in stark contrast. Lucia's mother was repelled by traditional practices of laying out the dead, all-night vigils, repeated rosary praying, as well as the post-funeral feasts with neighbors and kin. Hispanic tradition mandated that the dead not be left alone for days, causing the home of the bereaved to be filled with feasting people and constant conversation as they waited to take a turn being with the deceased. Lucia's mother wanted nothing to do with it. Children were an integral part of this tradition. Her child would not be seeing or, worse yet, touching any dead bodies. She would shield her child from this primitive and uncivilized practice.

Lucia was well into her twenties when her grandmother died. Numbed by grief, Lucia remained immersed in the Gringo way of her mother's Anglo culture and kept her emotional distance from the Hispanic death traditions, thus being spared *all of that barbarianism*. Years later Lucia looked back with regret. Not until in her forties would she participate *Nuevo Mexicano* style when her aunt, known affectionately as Mama Mary, passed away. The entire family took over the hospital room for the two weeks it took Mama Mary to die. Uncle Leo set the schedule to assure that someone sat with her around the clock, leaving no chance for hospital staff to forget her or mess up her care. Relatives came to sit and visit, to share stories and gossip, and to say good-bye. Lucia remembers standing as one of the family at bedside when Mama Mary spoke out *Parecen zopilotes!* meaning *You look like vultures!* The vitality of life has a way of finding its voice even death. Mama Mary slipped away in the wee hours with only Uncle Leo there. Women closest to Mama Mary went to the funeral home and made her up using their own bags of cosmetics, a final act of honoring one who was deeply loved.

Participation in Mama Mary's death vigil was a first for Lucia, an unforgettable, transformative experience and profound life lesson. She learned to be with death up close as a part of a collectivity, experiencing her grief deeply and beautifully. When Lucia's mother was dying, Lucia told her that she wanted to have people with her so she would not be alone. Following Uncle Leo's guide, Lucia scheduled her mother's final days, and her mother, who had vigorously rejected these customs she had considered uncivilized, shifted. Realizing the value of her daughter's concern and thoughtfulness, Lucia's mother was profoundly grateful.

While rituals are embedded in cultures and religions, there are times when they arise spontaneously. Delores[43] lost her sister Joanna, who died at 41 following a troubled life. Delores had always tried to protect her. The night after Joanna's death, Delores had a vivid dream: She was carrying her sister toward an indescribably beautiful light. A man in a long white robe emerged, walked toward them, and then reached out, taking Joanna in his arms. Placing her by his side, he took her hand and together they walked toward the light. In her dream, Delores sent a message as she watched them go. "I must go back now. You are safe. I will always love you." It was in that dream that she had been there for her sister one last time.

Delores shared her dream with friends and began receiving calls. Would she come talk with a young woman who is dying; be with another who is dying and terrified; spend time with a woman in critical condition? She would. Again and again, the questions were asked: Am I going to die? When am I going to die? Delores always responded that she did not know.

"The time is set between you and your God. Just know that when the time comes, I will pray to God to send you light."

Her words brought peace. When a woman, critical after open-heart surgery, wanted Delores to tell her if she were dying, Delores replied, "As long as you are breathing, you are alive. Breathe deeply and slowly." They were perfect words spoken at the perfect time. The two breathed in rhythm together until the woman became calm. Simple, unplanned sharing of wisdom replaced fear with peace. These stories point to the great need people have for information about death and our wanting someone we feel knows about death to be with us.

The dying have a greater need for emotional and spiritual care than they have for additional tests and treatment when both are futile. During the final stages of life, people need connection with people. They need social support and comfort. They need spiritual support. They need not be alone. Finding this ambiance in a hospital is an anomaly. The number of people opting to die at home or in a hospice-like facility is on the increase. We are learning how to help families provide the possibility for a sacred and dignified death, assuaging fears while providing comfort along with emotional and spiritual support. Amid candlelight, music, and prayer, feelings are shared, tears shed, stories told, gracious acts acknowledged and trespasses forgiven. Here death comes as an expected visitor. Here, it is a sacred passage, not a medical case.

To increase the possibility of being in a setting where one's wishes for a more peaceful death will be honored, paperwork stating the desires of the dying is essential. Hospital hierarchies must follow rigid policies. Without written instructions, heroic measures are usually taken. Without written directives on file, the concerned and grieving family may be called upon to make decisions on the spot. First find out if your family concurs with your wishes. Name a supportive person to see that those wishes are followed.

Do not leave a grieving and divided family with the burden of making painful, emotional decisions. Without a directive or a family member available, Code Blue is usually triggered, setting in motion the *Western Society's Ritual of Death*. The patient is rushed to ICU. Stimulants are mainlined into resistant veins. A tube is forced down the throat and air is pumped into dying lungs. The body convulses as the failing heart is repeatedly shocked in attempts to bring it alive. One can only, one can only imagine the terror and pain the patient must be feeling.

While we neither know nor can dictate how our final hours will play out, the choice to determine the setting where we will die can be ours. With the proper paperwork in order, there's good chance that those decisions will be honored. But the signed paperwork must be in order! I hear people say emphatically that they do not want to be kept alive on tubes and machines. Although many are passionate about how they wish to spend their final weeks or days, I have often heard the statement "If that happens to me, just pull the plug." People think that verbalizing their wishes takes care of every thing. It is not that easy! One can't walk into a hospital and start pulling out IVs and breathing machines because "that's what she said she wanted!" The law calls it murder.

My documents are in order. Between now and when they're needed, there is living to be done. When my death comes, I plan on being ready to make the trip. Until then, I bask in life playing out all around me. Dawn births a new day. At sunset the day is over. Spring comes alive with new birth. Irises, born anew each spring, share their glory and are gone. Rosebuds hold their potential tightly and then open to join roses in bloom. Blooms shrivel and drop away, leaving in their place seed-holding hips. It is the drama of life, each stage as significant as any other.

CHAPTER THIRTEEN

SEARCHING FOR THE SACRED

Approaching death has brought a heightened engagement with the Sacred. The basic premises of the array of religious and spiritual beliefs differ. Christianity, one of the world's major religions, is divided into Catholics and Protestants. Protestant churches include a vast number of major and minor denominations. Within these, members hold widely different tenets and ways for making personal connection with God. While most agree that life is followed by an afterlife, details differ widely regarding that afterlife, as are ways of getting there. By following specific and exclusive rules and rites—and there are many—it is not uncommon for groups to consider themselves the *only* group allowed entrance into the *Sacred Place* where souls continue to live after their bodies die. Non-believers are redirected to a much less desirable location.

Devotion to one's personal church involves loyalty to its teaching, which in turn, increases this sense of righteousness or superiority for one's own belief system and distain for the beliefs of others. Individual religions tend to consider themselves the *Chosen Ones* with each believing that their way is the only true way. Attitudes of being superior to the beliefs of others are at times less than loving. Wars are waged and masses are slaughtered over differing religions. Both historically and now, our lives are rife with violence as a result of our differing belief systems. Fortunately, many share an acceptance and respect for the beliefs of others, and this acceptance furthers harmony and peace. Throughout any search for the Sacred, one will find that the priorities of various religious groups have ranged from violence and cruelty to compassionate service dedicated to serving others. Each seeker finds a spiritual path that resonates with the seeker's inner needs.

Numinous experiences have played significant roles in the spiritual journeys of many. Lionel Corbett described the numinous as a "direct intuitive awareness of the transcendent realm.[44] Reading his words brought memories of an incident that took place well over a half-century ago, and with that memory came the realization that it had been a numinous experience. I was six, maybe seven years old. Sitting in the pasture grass waiting for my father to finish tending the horses, I watched the dirt moving, a sign of a diligent gopher working nearby. Suddenly, I was in a space of great clarity and knew in that instant that the dirt and the gopher and the grasses and the small stones and I were somehow made out of the same stuff. I was connected to everything. The experience lasted for the briefest moment but made an indelible impact. It was a gift from nowhere, and I questioned neither its authenticity nor its source. Nor did I tell anyone. I knew I held a secret.

Being connected with nature, like being one with the grasses, was just there—a feeling never associated with anything religious. I associated everything religious with my grandmother. She was a Christian and was determined to save me. Years later the realization came that my grandmother was protecting me from what she saw as evil in the only way she knew how to protect me. At the time, I was impatient with her fussing and felt that I was being unfairly picked on. Just before my wedding, I made some comment about Grandma's criticism, and my mother explained my grandma worried about me because I was her favorite. "She gave you her gold watch. She told me that you are to get the clock. She frets over you because she wants you to be safe." Her comments surprised me and pleased me. I had no idea. As an adult I am deeply moved to know how much she loved me.

My father's religious expression was quite different from Grandma's. He was saved by Christian Fundamentalists during his first year at U.C. Berkeley in the 1920s but abandoned his newly found faith shortly thereafter. Subsequently his reference to Jesus or God was limited to *gee-sus key-riste goddamned-sonofabitch!*—a brief sermon often repeated in angry intensity and clearly devoid of reverence. My problematic relationship with him was complex. My fear of him fueled a dislike bordering on hatred and served as a defense against his rages. In time my anger released, and I declared a truce, but by then, he had been dead for twenty years.

Today, I am surprised to find that I can remember valuable things about my father that ranged from the small and trivial to the significant and influential, which I had previously ignored, even though they had had a positive impact on my life. While I remained relieved to have him out of my life, the bitter clouds of anger have abated, and

I feel surprisingly compassionate for his struggles and traumatic childhood. To be able to look at these re-assessed memories as gifts eased the intensity of my anger. My connection with my mother was warm and nurturing. A deeply spiritual woman, she was caught between a husband she both feared and felt compassion for and a mother whose focus on sin she rejected. I remember Mama tucking me into bed, bending close, one arm cradling my head as she whispered the Lord's Prayer or the Twenty-third Psalm in my ear. I felt safe and warm and loved. Night after night, her voice like hushed music, my mother shared her vision of a gentle God, laying the groundwork for me to ultimately find peace with the Sacred.

When I was nine, the Salvation Army held Sunday school at a neighbor's house. I went because my friend went and because they served cookies and Kool-Aid. There I learned that God knew every bird that flew in the sky, how many hairs grew on each person's head, and that He could move mountains. Being simultaneously impressed and skeptical, I climbed up onto the bathroom counter so I could see up close in the mirror and started counting the hairs in my bangs. It immediately became clear that it would be easier if I were to ask God to move the mountains. Nestled into my favorite hiding place out of sight behind the Eugenia hedge at the top of a slope covered with yellow-flowered lantana. There I had flattened a space to make a small nest for myself. To be sure I left no trail so no one could find me, I made my way stealthily, lifting my feet high with each step so as not to create a path. A path, would give away my secret place. Often, I would curl up in my nest and remain motionless, pretending to be a fawn in the forest. I loved pretending to be a wild fawn.

From this secret place, I could see the Sierra Madre Mountains. Sitting still and using my best manners, I made my request to God to please move the mountains. Closing my eyes I waited. The mountains stood fixed. I asked again, this time saying please twice. Again nothing. My disappointment was huge. The Captains from the Salvation Army were nice people, but cookies or no cookies, it was clear that I could not believe them. Oblivious of metaphor, I knew nothing about moving the mountains of the soul.

During high school I became embroiled in a mix of religious teachings and continued to encounter an angry, punitive God whom I was asked to simultaneously worship and fear. I was told that I had free choice, and then chastised if I exercised that choice. I felt bribed and threatened. Believe as they believe, and I would live in the Paradise of Heaven forever. Differ, and I would burn in Hell. In my early teenage years, one of the ministers took special interest in me and volunteered to give me individualized counseling in my search for God. After several sessions he became inappropriately cozy. He slipped his arms around me from behind, one hand covering a small breast and the other holding my head against his chest as he breathed heavily into my ear. I had the presence of mind to scream, "Let go of me or my father will kill you!" My father was well known in the area, and the young minister dropped me like a hot potato. In truth, I was afraid that my father would kill me. I said not a word about the incident and never returned to that church.

In high school I attended the local Methodist Church, where the mesmerizing young minister won everyone over. My group of friends and I were his ardent fans. I had found my religious home. His sermons were filled with inspiring parables, many of which remain with me today. I was baptized the following year when I was seventeen, but not in my church. I was spending the summer with my grandmother in Oakland, California, and in my teenage urge to please her, agreed to be baptized in her church. After all, I was now religious and could be baptized in good conscience.

Meeting the minister at Grandma's church for the first time, I didn't like him. He was stern and authoritarian. There was no greeting. He mentioned nothing about being pleased that I had found Christ, nothing about how wonderful it was that my baptism was going to save me from the fires of Hell. Nothing. His first statement: Baptism must be done by submersion. That's the only way you can get into Heaven. I cautiously explained that it didn't matter to me whether I was submerged or sprinkled with Holy Water. For me, what mattered was the way I felt about God. Wham! He looked at me fiercely and said, "Young lady, your grandma wants you baptized, and we are going to do it The-Right-Way!"

Shaken, a bit frightened, and feeling less than spiritual, I changed into the baptismal robe, a sort of white hospital gown with better coverage in the rear. A kindly woman asked if I wanted a bathing cap. "So you won't mess up your hair." I said, "If I'm being submerged, I might as well get my head baptized, too." Attired appropriately, I entered the baptismal room. The assistant minister standing waist deep in the waters of the baptismal tub startled me. He was humongous, ruddy-faced, and wore a white gown like mine, but much larger, the fabric of which floated out onto the water. I hoped fervently that he wore something underneath and was fast having second thoughts about being baptized.

Three of us waited to be saved from the Eternal Fires. I went first. The huge man held me under my back, and placing his bulbous hand over my face, mumbled something about Jesus Christ and dipped me totally but briefly into the Holy Water. It took seconds. Someone offered a hand to help me out of the water. I was now a Christian and felt empty and confused. Changing my clothes and pulling my dripping hair into a ponytail, I made sure to hug my grandma and grandpa before leaving for the bus. Grandma beamed. Grandpa smiled. I left. Once on the bus, I rode in silence to Edy's Ice Cream Parlor near Lake Merritt where I waited tables.

That fall I started college, abandoned the terrifying, white-bearded Father God of Christianity, recoiled at even hearing the word *God*, and proceeded to embrace nothing, which didn't work for me either. Having flailed about for years trying to find *It* somewhere *out there*, I found that all along *It* was within me. I began to reopen to the possibility finding the Sacred, the part of each of us and of all of us that holds a part of God. The Oneness and Everywhereness of my God-ness grew stronger. Bit by bit, I breathed *It* in. At times *It* pulsed through my veins. I recognized *It* in the face of a child, in the wind blowing through trees, in the magic of birds, and in the dawn of a day.

This seeping-in of a new consciousness came in fragments and fed me. These scraps, the makings of Psyche's ultimate Stone Soup of children's stories—a metaphoric stone, a carrot, a potato, a pinch of salt—contained insights and pieces of wisdom offered up from each of us and added to the soup of consciousness from which all of us can feed. Awareness that God is everywhere—in all things, in me—seeped into me as though by osmosis. My search did not include thinking it through. It was not a matter of figuring it out. The Sacred was not coming to me via the brain. The Sacred quietly instilled itself, setting up residence and bringing me comfort.

CHAPTER FOURTEEN

FALLING AND GETTING BACK UP

Having experienced this shift in my connection with things Sacred, I was freed of the longing that had played an intrinsic role in my life and in propelling my on-going search. The shift from seeking to finding brought significant peace. Being part of and connected with the Sacred was difficult to explain, since nothing dramatic had happened. No single incident took place. Neither dogma nor structure were involved. On those few occasions when I tried to share, I was met with confused looks followed by eagerness on the part of others to share their clearly spelled out church tenants. Enthusiastic invitations for me to join their churches were common. Keeping my mouth shut seemed prudent, and I kept my feelings and conclusions to myself. Without the nourishing attention that anything needs in order to grow and thrive, and in the context of life's pressing demands, my theology gradually moved to the back burners of my daily life waiting to be called forth when needed.

Life for me unfolded much as the lives of others of my era and circumstance. I married, taught school, raised my three children, wrote and published educational materials, fixed dinner, did the laundry, cleaned the toilet, and worked in my flower garden, drove my kids to their dental appointments. The genius of the man I married lay in the worlds of mathematics and engineering, neither of which I truly understood. When not working, his interest was in watching our newest acquisition, television, which held little appeal for me. His philosophical thoughts, opinions, and feelings were left unsaid, and my chatter and yearnings to share everything were met with annoyance. In the end, we shared a home, a bed, and children. Neither of us had the skills to bridge the gap, allowing for an emotional vacuum between us to develop and flourish. Eventually, we divorced. The realm of the sacred or religion in any formal sense did not touch our household.

This situation was made clear by my children's comments. My first-grade daughter's Jewish friend attended Saturday school. Her Catholic friend attended Catechism. Another good friend went to the Presbyterian Church and attended Sunday school. When she was asked what her religion was, my daughter looked a bit confused and then answered, "Public, I guess." She did, after all, attend public school.

My oldest son was the religious advisor to his younger brother. Our home on the north side of the Palos Verdes Peninsula overlooked the ocean and the cities from Los Angeles to Malibu. In their early morning ritual, the two boys would come running up the stairs and onto the deck to check out the surf. Then it was a dash to the phone in the kitchen to check with friends who had views of different surfing spots. A decision was made, and they were off and into the water shortly after dawn to catch a few waves before school. Following late afternoon surfing, they would climb the cliffs of Malaga Cove, surfboards atop their heads, and take a short cut through the churchyard of Haggerty's Church, where youth groups were playing volleyball.

One evening my youngest son asked his older brother what a church was. My worldly, well-informed, and all-knowing twelve-year-old explained that church was where people played volleyball. Listening to the conversation, my mother said that it wouldn't hurt them to have at least some information about churches and religion. She was probably right, although the kids all grew up to be responsible, caring, kind, and ethical adults.

After leaving a twenty-year marriage, I returned to teaching and writing. Two years later, I decided to become self-employed. It was a huge step, but my ignorance of what was involved in going out on one's own precluded my having the good sense to be worried. Somehow, I managed to round-up a conglomeration of odd jobs: writing a funding proposal for a start-up, a training program for a small business, editing a company handbook, giving a speech here, a speech there, writing speeches for others.

I had no difficulty doing the work; the skill for collecting my earnings was nil. I was running pell-mell at full speed in circles and knew that something had to change, that I needed to stop and take stock of my life.

I would stop. Yes, just as soon as I finished the current project. Earning a living took precedence. Listening to my gut did not. Thoughts of the Sacred were nowhere near. Number one on the list was buying groceries. Then came the fall down the stairs that turned my life upside down.

Shortly after 5:00 in the morning on May 19, 1971, I put on a pot of coffee and walked back toward the bedroom. In the foyer at the top of the stairs leading down to the children's bedrooms, I turned my ankle and fell backward into the stairwell. For a terrifying instant I touched nothing before hitting stairs, tumbling over and over until finally landing against the wrought-iron railing at bottom. Lying motionless in a broken heap, my first thought was that I had to find why this happened. My next thought was that I would lose everything, including my home if I couldn't work. Then I thought *at least I'm not married.*

Derek, my youngest son who had recently turned fourteen, heard the commotion of my fall and came to investigate. He reached down and picked me up, held me at the waist and carried me effortlessly up the stairs, holding me in front of him. I felt weightless. Later he told me that it was very strange. When he picked me up, it seemed like I didn't weigh anything, like I was a doll. Brad had joined us. The boys wanted to know what to do next. I told them to put me down on the corner of the bed and that I needed a minute to think. After a few minutes, I asked them to pull back the collar of my pajamas and see if anything was broken. I don't know who spoke. The answer was "Yes, Mama, something is broken." They took me to the emergency room.

After being hospitalized for two weeks due, not only to injuries but also to treat the blood clots that had developed, I was released to recuperate at home for the next three months, which gave me plenty of time to reassess my life. When I finally was able to work again, my life and business took a new and eventually profitable direction. I started out with a woman coming into my home office two or three hours a week to type. When West Bristow Consultants was sold ten years later, we had twelve full-time people and from forty to fifty contract professionals. Gloria, the woman who had once typed for me, became a phenomenal driving force for our success. She ran the nuts and bolts of the day-to-day operations and no longer had a typewriter in her office. I could not fathom making it all work without her. But I am getting ahead of myself.

While recovering, my back would spasm at night. Every two or three hours, I would get up and walk around the house, around the couches that sat well away from the walls in the living room, through the dining room and around the table, and then out onto the deck. Around and around, I walked until the spasms eased. During this time, I was reading Carl Jung's *Man and His Symbols*. In it, Jung wrote of his studying the religious practices of indigenous people. Camped just outside of the village of an African tribe, and with a translator, Jung asked them about their religion. They said they didn't have any. However, at dawn every morning, they would stand together, blow or spit into their hands and raise them toward the breaking sun. Jung compared this ritual to other religions, breath as spirit; spittle as life's substance. "Unto thy hands I commend my spirit" is a universal prayer.

It was late in June, and while I diligently did the exercises given me by the physical therapist, my right arm and hand remained useless. Due to my routine of nightly strolls throughout the house and onto the deck, I was usually awake at dawn. June mornings in Southern California are invariably foggy, but morning after morning during June of 1971, the mornings dawned clear. I loved watching the sunrise, the opening ceremony for a new day, but greeting the dawn on this particular day brought no joy. I was losing hope that my arm and hand would heal in time for me to be able to work. Without being able to work, how could I keep my life together or keep my kids in this house. This sunrise heralded another day of no progress. The new days arrived, each bringing another day of wondering how I could survive.

Depressed and helpless, I watched intently as the eastern sky began to lighten and then color. Finally, the mighty sun made its entrance. Staring at it intensely and without forethought, I slowly, slowly lifted my left hand to my face, blew cautiously into my palm and tenuously raised it to the coming sun. Tears streaming down my face, I whispered, "Unto thy hands I commend my spirit." Over two decades after my baptism-by-submersion and not quite consciously, for a wrathful God and my father remained entwined, alone on the deck of the Via Somonte house, I made connection with the Sacred and gave myself to an unknown God.

Mostly life goes on and we all do what everyone does and that is the stuff that needs to be done. I have learned to move through pain as I move through euphoria, drinking and breathing in the substance of experience, emerging from pain stronger and wiser, from joy, richer. I know now that for me the Essence of God is the Essence of Life, and I am, as is all life, of that Essence. The Essence does not die.

CHAPTER FIFTEEN

DYING: A NEW PARADIGM

It is time for a paradigm shift, time for us to take a compassionate, in-depth, and intelligent look at our society's ways of dealing with death. Our current attempts to defeat death when death is imminent are costly and accomplish nothing. If this same activity were not conducted in a hospital under the auspices of helping a person live, it could easily be considered torture. Our approach to end-of-life care is propelled by fears of aging and dying and guilt. We want society to approve of what we do. What if other people think we didn't do enough to save a loved one? Both doctors and families find comfort when they feel that everything possible was done to prolong someone's life, even when that someone had no chance for survival. Acquiescing to the cultural norm, we tend to settle comfortably into the status quo. Going against the accepted way of doing things often causes the ruffling of society's feathers. For decades, any mention or meaningful discussion of different perspectives on life and death has created such ruffling.

In a medical crisis, the first action taken is to rush the individual to the nearest ER. Medical personnel, highly trained in dealing with medical crises, provide what they see as necessary and appropriate intervention. There is a high probability that the person will survive, get well, and return to a normal life but when an individual is in the final stages of life and no cure is possible, invasive intervention is not appropriate. The crisis mode present in emergency rooms is necessary. The emergency room is there to handle emergencies. The challenge is to make the assessment and take steps so that medical treatment is provided or withheld appropriately. Rarely has consideration been given to a plan for alternative actions. How does one know for sure who goes to emergency or who remains at home? Preparation is crucial. Before the decision has to be made regarding treatment, a person's preference needs to be known. Gently open a conversation with the one who is either elderly or unwell, share your love for them, and explain that you want to do whatever it is that the person wants to have done. Ask about that person's wishes. If that is not possible, meet with family members or dear friends and determine a plan for the final days. Having a plan in place guides the caregiver in knowing whether to call 911 or the family. If an individual has planned ahead, has directives in place, and has told her wishes to family and friends, the decision to keep her at home is not difficult. The number of individuals who are putting their wishes in writing is on the increase, but society still has a long way to go.

Planning needs to include the actions to be taken as someone nears death. Whom do you notify? Have arrangements been made to have a person there to help the family through this difficult time? What arrangements have been made for creating a peaceful environment and for easing pain? Whom do you call for support if support is needed? The hospital is not the place to have a reasonably calm and comfortable death. A peaceful death has a better chance of happening when one dies at home.

Changes are challenging, necessary, and most are eventually unavoidable. They are especially sticky when being introduced in an emotionally charged situation. The activities surrounding death, including making arrangements for the funeral, are definitely charged. In 1963, Jessica Mitford's book, *The American Way of Dying*,[45] focused on the funeral industry and challenged us to question how the business was being conducted. Funerals reflect another aspect of our distorted relationship with death. Preying on a family's guilt or vulnerability, skilled sales people trained in zeroing in on sensitive emotional issues use subtle yet powerful pressures to sell more than is needed. Elaborate caskets reflect guilt as often as love and respect. Confusion and guilt leave mourners defenseless. How selfish would it be to question the costs of a loved one's burial? How can one not demonstrate their love and respect for the dead? What would people think if we failed to provide an elegant casket and funeral for our wonderful Aunt Mabel? Everyone knows how she loved beautiful things. Who could be so crass as to haggle over the cost of Grandpa's casket? Hadn't he lived an honorable life? Hadn't he served his country as a soldier during the war? Certainly he deserved to be honored appropriately—and expensively. Mitford's book demanded that we look squarely at our American way of dying and inspired us to make a shift in our attitudes and actions.

The next major influence on our attitudes toward death came in 1970 when Elizabeth Kübler Ross jolted people awake with her revolutionary book, *On Death and Dying*.[46] Her courage, or for some, her audacity to look directly at death surprised us, intrigued us, shocked us, and helped us change. Whatever our reactions, we flocked to read the book and are still reading it today. Today, we are also looking at the final stages of life and how we are addressing death. We are asking if there isn't a better way. Today's medical expertise can work miracles and often does. Many live today because of the dedication and expertise of a team of medical professionals. Yet there is another side of medical care that the medical professionals, institutions, as well as individuals are beginning to assess and address. How are we are going to deal with our practice of prolonging lives during the final months, weeks, and even days when there is no possibility of being cured? The use of fruitless, painful and frightening measures when an individual is dying, helpless, and unable to object is cruel. Are those measures justified? Is it fair or compassionate to subject a dying person to violent treatment that cannot help him? When one's quality of life is marginal at best and miserable in many cases, when there is no chance for recovery, is it caring or even reasonable to subject someone to additional and unnecessary suffering? Do we have the right to deny or marginalize a person's opportunity to have a dignified death? And then, of course, there is the astronomical cost of hospital care that threatens the stability of our nation's economy.

Horror stories abound. When a ninety-two-year-old collapsed at home, his wife called the paramedics, who arrived and continued to apply CPR for over an hour. Looking at death through the lens of the spirit of the shaman, attempting to resuscitate a person who has just died or who is dying appears barbaric.

My neighbor's mother was terminally ill and once again being rushed to the hospital. The pattern of going to the hospital, receiving treatment that would buy her a little time, and then being sent home had been going on for over a year. Now another crisis, another rush to the hospital, another seven days while extreme measures kept her alive. Again she came home. This time she died. The last year of her life was miserable. She was helpless, under heavy medication, constantly complaining, and angry. Her daughter commented, "We've been on the 365/365 program now for over a year—365 days a year at $365 a day for round-the-clock care! I don't understand it. It doesn't make sense. Our boys will start college in a year or so and that money could go to pay expenses."

When an elderly man was seriously injured in a fall, he was rushed to the hospital and stabilized. Casts supported his broken bones, including his neck and back. His prognosis was dire. Heavy smoking and drinking during years of an inactive life had left his body in extremely poor condition. His lungs were failing, his liver had been severely damaged, his kidneys functioned poorly, and his intestines were riddled with perforations. His condition worsened after the accident. Although intestinal bleeding called for surgery, doctors doubted he could survive and advised against it. His wife insisted it be done. He survived the removal of much of his intestines, as well as the placement of a pacemaker to stabilize an erratic heart. The doctors discouraged further emergency treatment. His wife insisted he stay on Code Blue. He was resuscitated several times. After weeks in intensive care, he was moved to a care facility for the terminally ill, hooked up to machines to do his breathing and pump his blood. All food was served intravenously. His body waste was deposited in a bag beside his bed. Due to the body casts, he could not move. He could barely speak. His wife visited him regularly. Generous supplementary insurance paid for her travel and hotel expenses. For over six months, she spent Monday mornings traveling to the care facility. Monday afternoons, Tuesdays and Wednesdays she spent with her husband. She visited a few hours on Thursday mornings before leaving for her trip home. Finally, her insurance policy reached its maximum coverage, and she realized she would be bankrupt within six months if she paid for his expenses and her visiting routine out of pocket. Without a word to her husband, she had life support discontinued. He died the next day.

A small town newspaper reported that an eighty-five-year-old grandfather, a highly respected, long-time resident, had a stroke and was hospitalized. Within days, a second stroke rendered him unable to speak. A third stroke left him comatose. His devoted family saw to it that he had the best of care. Paying medical costs not covered by Medicare rapidly depleted their life's savings as well as the mortgage they took out on their home. Their grandfather lived in a coma for a year. Unable to make the payments, his widow lost their home in foreclosure. Did grandfather want this?

I see people carrying signs reading "Don't Kill Grandma!" I am grandmother and a great-grandmother, and I want to call out, "You are mistaken! Honor your grandmother. When your grandma is dying and helpless, save her from painful treatments that don't work. Allow her to go with blessings when her God calls for her."

For the terminally ill in the final stages of life, harsh, hurtful treatments cause great suffering. They do not bring dying patients back to health or prevent the certainty of death. Many don't want artificially sustained, marginal lives. For others, the decision to cease treatment is an indication that the family doesn't express sufficient love. Often people are not prepared to make such a difficult decision. Regardless of where or when we die, let us imagine for a moment that the soul is able to view the birth-life-death cycle from some omniscient place. Would one not experience greater fear of facing birth than of facing death? Imagine hours of being squeezed through a narrow channel as you are being expelled from the warm comfort of the mother's womb. After that, you enter a life filled with stress, frustration, suffering, and struggle. Death may have its hours of pain, but life's pain comes and goes over a lifespan. In death there is also the possibility of coming home to wholeness. Heaven, Nirvana, Paradise, all offer enticing images. Stories of near-death experiences share visions of a tunnel of light leading to a place of indescribable peace.

Dr. Alberto Villoldo[47] believes that a peaceful death is the most precious gift that we can offer a loved one. Machines repeatedly shocking our dying hearts and tubes forced down our throats do not make for peaceful transitions. When I am ready to die, let me die. Years ago, discussing the issue of my death, I discovered that my doctor was committed to saving lives at all costs. I found another doctor. No tubes will be inserted into every orifice of my body, no machines for breathing or pumping blood. I want to die at home with loved ones, be as free of pain as possible, and be present at my death.

My life expectancy has come and gone. Death hovers ever more closely; will it arrive in a decade, maybe later, maybe sooner, maybe tomorrow? Shamanic teaching states that when a dying person retains awareness, he enters the light more easily. Many do. I may or may not. Soul work continues. For now, I nurture awareness as I entertain thoughts of entering the light with relative ease. My plan is to leave directly from home.

CHAPTER SIXTEEN
WALKING EACH DAY WITH DEATH

Death, Thanatos, walks each step with me and is no longer an enemy to fear. I prefer to see him as the Greeks saw him, here to carry us through death when our time comes rather than the harsh and cruel god of mythology or the death drive he symbolizes in the field of psychology. Having him near brings me comfort, much as it is comforting to have a guide along who knows the territory when I am visiting an unfamiliar and perhaps frightening place. Thanatos is invited to accompany me when it is time for me to journey into the ultimate unknown.

According to Dr. Michael Kearney,[48] author of *Mortally Wounded*, a current dilemma in Western society is that we live our lives largely separated from soul. He tells us that, on one hand, soul is the living connection between the surface mind and the unfathomable, meaning-rich depths of who we are. On the other hand, the ego finds expression with things of the surface mind and wants nothing to do with a descent into the core of our beings. Ego is afraid of death. Soul walks with Thanatos. Neither is afraid. However, in spite of our efforts in our everyday lives to rise above fear, our egos are adept at taking control. As they do, our fears thrive.

The gods of magazines and miracle products coalesce in an amalgam of pseudo-science, fundamental dogma, hocus-pocus, and materialism. Soul is left to fend for herself, while our collective ennui has us ingesting happy pills and sedatives in an attempts to find meaning and purpose. We cram stuff into our insatiable cores of emptiness. We change our bodies and faces to comply with anonymous marketers' composites of the acceptable image of beauty. Their edict: We must not get old. We must not get fat. We must not be unhappy. We must not die. Accomplish the first three, and we will still die. Death, which is potentially the ultimate transformative process and certainly the final experience of one's current life, is commonly associated with fear-laden darkness. It is important to remember, however, that death is also associated with peace and joy and love, especially among octogenarians. For us, a calming and serene peace accompanies our acceptance of the inevitable. It is the soul's version of being on speaking terms with what the personality has long denied.

 I grew up in the semi-rural Southern California of the 1930s. In our neighborhood, we saw birth and death as natural occurrences to be treated as honored events. No heroic measures were available to wage battle against death during one's last hours. Death was tragic when it caused a loss or hardship to the surviving family or when one was young or in the prime of life. Those who died young ruptured the flow of our accepted rhythm of life. When an elderly person passed away, a stoic demeanor signaled acceptance of the reality of death. Simple funerals were often held in small homes where family and friends squeezed together solemnly paying their respects.

When my grandmother died in her mid 90s during the mid 1950s, the funeral home director suggested that we honor Grandmother by purchasing their most expensive casket "so that her friends would know how much her family valued and loved her." My skin crawled in reaction to his condescending comment and his unctuous demeanor. My brother was quick to respond, saying that her friends were dead, and she was a nice grandma, but we did not need a fancy casket. I wanted to shout my approval, but didn't have the courage. At church, fewer than twenty people gathered, mostly family. The service was short and simple. We gathered again at Grandma's house, ate food fixed by relatives, and talked about what a wonderful Grandma she was. We would miss her. Hers had been a peaceful and dignified death.

Decades passed before I understood what a remarkable woman she was. Going through a box of her letters written in pencil in precise handwriting on now-yellowed, lined pages taken from a tablet of writing paper, I was surprised and intrigued by what she wrote. Only then did I begin to understand her courage and her depth. She saw drunkenness as a scourge against women and children, as indeed it was. Husbands and fathers took their Friday pay to the local bar, returning home penniless, drunk, and angry, to rage at their hungry families. (My grandfather, bless his heart, was a gentle soul. Never had I seen or heard of him consuming alcohol. Maybe he didn't dare!)

Grandma also wrote of the injustice of women being forbidden to vote, but I am sure she wielded a significant influence on my grandfather's vote. I knew nothing of her thoughts or feelings on issues other than religion, which contributed to our lack of closeness. Learning that we shared deep commitments, I felt closer to her now even though she had died years before. I shared her outrage. I always thought of women not having the right to vote as something existing in the distant past. The movement started in the 1700s, but the Nineteenth Amendment did not become law until 1920, and then by a single vote. The date had not resonated with me before reading her letter, at which time I realized that women were not able to vote until nine years before I was born. Nine years is less than a decade, a blink of an eye in time. Her letters opened the possibility that we might have had a connection other than the one we did have. I would never know, but what but what did happen is that my memory of her shifted to incorporate the possibility of a deeper bond. Learning late of her convictions certainly shifted how I see her now. I wish I had known how she felt before she died. I would have loved to share our thoughts. But at her funeral on that long ago sunny afternoon in 1955, I thought of her as hardworking and loving, but perhaps a bit strict.

Funerals have changed with time. A half-century later, an acquaintance of mine died after a brief illness.

She had led an active life in her community. In contrast to that of my grandmother, the funeral was an orchestrated production: a small, private service for the family followed by a sumptuous spread in their lovely Brentwood home for about eighty family members and close friends. Days later a public service was held for community members in a church that could accommodate about six hundred attendees. City dignitaries and a few minor celebrities spoke, a professionally done video production of her active life was shown, and a small, locally well-known chorus sang several of her favorite songs. The service ended with the usual pigeon-dove scenario in which the image of gentle doves flying skyward as sacred escorts for the departing soul was obliterated by the frenetic flapping of the wings of hungry pigeons rented for the occasion. Few mourners noticed as they burst raucously from their cage and flew home for supper. Everyone cried, even those with only a passing acquaintance with the woman.

I wondered if elaborate funerals were the new in-thing. Were extravagant funerals an attempt to make death more palatable? Are they held to amplify the celebrity aspect of one's life? Are ostentatious and expensive funerals, like weddings, becoming displays of status? Of love? Of respect? Or in fear of what others might think or say? I left with an empty feeling in the pit of my stomach.

After the funeral, uncomfortable and diffused feelings continued to haunt me. Memories of small funerals followed by a potluck spread held in a neighbor's home replayed in my mind. What became clear was that when I died, I would have something simple if I had anything at all—maybe some champagne in the garden with a few close friends and my immediate family. Perhaps they could sprinkle my ashes in the perennial garden that has brought me much joy. Perhaps someone can quote Maya Angelou as she answers the heroic question, "Death, where is thy sting? It is here in my heart and mind and memories."[49] She does not mention fear.

The thought of living until senility consumes my mind and helplessness steals my body holds no appeal. Over time, I have reframed my death into a transition from the known to the unknown—a continuation of the same process my life has undergone. Following the shaman's belief that attitudes in facing and moving into death affect how the death passage unfolds, I am more determined than ever that, when my time comes, I want to be prepared, present, and conscious. I resonate with the words of Montaigne: "A lifelong acquaintance with the ways of death will soften one's final hours."[50]

A particularly enlightening experience on my journey was a four-day workshop called *Dying Consciously: The Greatest Journey* offered by the Four Winds Society. This workshop taps the ancient energy medicine of the Inka and the shamanic rituals for the dying. Participating in a shamanic ceremony of death, we ceremonialize our deaths in a beautiful and moving way. Fear is absent. Participating in these rituals illuminated my understanding of the journey and deepened my desire to meet, embrace, and move into my death.

In life we seek wholeness. With time facets of consciousness that make up wholeness accrue. We gather consciousness as we gather stones along life's paths. As I gathered stones, my life changed. The dying became my teachers. Acceptance of death's coming frees me to spend my time and energy connecting with the vitality and wonder of my life.

CHAPTER SEVENTEEN
THE LAST DANCE

While the story of growing soul is everyone's story, it is at the same time uniquely yours as it is uniquely his or hers or mine. For many, peace with death is found through religious faith. Others who are deeply religious remain caught up in fear. Questions abound. Facing death is integral to this story. Gathering a library of readings offers a foundation from which to launch a search for information, understanding, and acceptance of death. We are not alone as we delve into the mystery of death's inevitability or encounter implications that trigger fear that causes us to pull away. We must not pull away. Our individual insights and instincts, as well as our thoughtful perceptions play key roles in the resolution of death's reality. Our capacity to trust plays another. In the end, there can come a calm and appreciative acceptance that in death, there is often a sense of coming home.

Molded by demands and rigors, by the pain and the joy, by the frenetic and the serene, my life experiences and reflections take narrative form, personal creations depicting life. These then become containers, the alchemist's crucible in which the transformative process of one's essence anneals and emerges. Too often the palimpsest of ego threatens; internecine jousting of old angers and fears consume precious energies. Attempts to write meaningfully about death tap into resources not only academically and intellectually but also, and for the most part, emotionally and spiritually. A mix of focus, reflection, and frustration is interspersed with periods of immense satisfaction. We find ourselves driven by intuition that exists in opposition to uneasy anxiety. The goal is to keep it all in balance. The reality is that the pendulum swings.

My heart sings to hear Jung's timeless theme, "I am and remain in search of myself, of the truth peculiar to myself."[51] As he searched the truth of himself, he also sought understanding of his death. Jung explained that, in the view of the ego, death could be frightening, capricious, and brutal, tearing away those we hold dear while we wait to be snatched from our lives at some arbitrary and unknowable time, leaving us angry and bitter. However, in the view of eternity, death appears as a joyous passage into the place where the soul gains wholeness and peace.

What one believes to be true about life usually parallels what one believes to be true about death. Perceptions and questions abound and intrigue us. Answers elude us. In our search for wholeness, we gather information, each in our own way. For me, the crone without her internal spirit child leaves my life incomplete. Through reflection they rise together toward wholeness. Separation falls away. The child, the young woman, the bride, the mother, the teacher, the professional, the mature woman, the grandmother and great-grandmother join the aging crone and meld into the creation of this old woman who at last is coming home to soul.

The poignant words of P.L. Travers capture the essence of death's resolution, "To be pregnant with one's death is to experience a surge of energy."[52] The writing of this book took my hand and led me through fears I did not know were there. I tried to clear the glass and peer through death's dark window. From time to time, I gently tapped at death's door cautiously seeking entry. Today, I stand at the edge of the River Styx at peace and dip my toe into the sacred essence, readying myself to move through darkness into ultimate light.

APPENDIX

The focus on old age sharpened as I approached the dissertation. Ultimately, my old age played a significant role in writing on the final stage of Jung's Individuation, a process that can continue into and through one's final years. By the time I defended my dissertation a short time after my eightieth birthday, the comfort and appreciation of old age had settled in. Peace with old age also brought peace with my death that waits nearby for me.

A definite pull drew me into working with Hospice. Volunteers spoke of the deep emotional rewards of bringing comfort to the dying, which played a major role in bringing consciousness of my death into my life. At last, it felt comforting to befriend Thanatos. The seeds for this book had been planted and grew this book about my journey toward accepting death's grace.

I found numerous books on old age and death offering a plethora of varying and valuable information, as well as differing opinions about the universal experience of dying. *Recommended Reading* lists some of those publications. New to me were the numerous organizations whose offerings meet and fulfill a multitude of needs relating to old age and end-of-life issues as someone approaches death. I knew of Hospice, of course, but the number of other organizations, both established and recently started surprised me. People are becoming interested in and curious about death and are brimming with questions. They want to know; they want information. At last, the taboos surrounding death are giving way.

My first intent in preparing this Appendix was to share the few groups I knew about and with whom I have had unusually positive experience in learning about death. In the process, I learned of many I had never heard of. The list included here just scratches the surface of available information and help. Its intent is to open a few doors, which in turn, might open more doors to material on all aspects of our end-of-life experiences. I trust this appendix can serve as a starting point in gathering information you are seeking.

• • • • • • • •

DYING CONSCIOUSLY: THE GREATEST JOURNEY

When I learned that the Four Winds Society was offering a workshop called Dying Consciously: The Greatest Journey, I knew that I must attend and have been forever grateful that I did. It was a life-changing experience. Fortunately, there are now trained individuals offering workshops throughout the USA, Canada, Europe, and Australia on a regular basis.

In working with the ancient energy of the Inka, this program helps participants help themselves and then help others find peace and closure with death, whether anticipating one's own death or dealing with the death of a loved one.

As part of the sessions, students participate in a shamanic ceremony of death, playing out their own deaths in a beautiful and moving way. Fear is absent. The experience is profound. My participation brought another shift in the resolution and understanding of my journey forward to meet, embrace, and move into my death.

Sharing the profound experience of enacting my own death awakened within me an indescribable knowing that, at a soul level, I was connected with something sacred and vast. Light, airy, joyous feelings filled me with a sense that all souls are connected to all souls, yet I remained simultaneously connected and separate. Death had become my companion and friend, woven into my life as integrally as my experiences and insights, joy and love, sorrow and pain.

While life is made up of myriad transformative experiences, the ultimate ones are birth and death, birth bringing us into life, death escorting us out. Facing the reality of my death brought comfort and acceptance. Dignity and peace came with roleplaying a simulation of the Shamanic death rites practiced from ancient times and still practiced today. Participation brought another shift in my journey toward moving into my death with grace. Comfort came with knowing that my embracing death as my companion and friend would help my children and grown grandchildren find peace when it comes my time to die.

For further information on Dying Consciously: The Greatest Journey contact:*

www.dyingconsciously.org

*For a state-by-state directory of Certified Teachers who offer workshops and training in *Dying Consciously: The Greatest Journey.*

http://www.dyingconsciously.org/DC-teachers.htm

• • • • • • • •

DEATH CAFÉ

Initially, I thought the name was a bit macabre and was somewhat taken aback when I first heard of the Death Café over lunch with Lynn Holtzman, the founder of the Santa Barbara Chapter. After attending the first meeting and learning more about it, the value of the Death Café became clear. Started in the UK, as were several other organizations addressing end-of-life issues, the Death Café is spreading quite rapidly throughout the United States, Europe, Canada, and Australia.

Historically, death has been a topic seldom mentioned in polite company, but that is changing. It turns out that people have questions about death and are reluctant or afraid to ask. They want to share feelings and fears and do not have anyone with whom to share those feelings. People want information about the experiences of others. They want information about what they can do. Unresolved feelings or unanswered questions about death abound.

People attend Death Café gatherings to be able to talk with and listen to others who are interested in talking about death. The situations are as varied and the people attending. From being terminally ill or having someone close to you who terminally ill, to have lost some one and are struggling with you pain, or just curious. Whatever it is regarding death is welcome conversation.

Sharing fears and feelings can make others uneasy. One frequently hears cheery words. "Do be so sad. You are going make it through this! Think positively!" or "Do 't be discouraged. Things are going to be all right!" or "You'll feel better soon. Keep a positive attitude." Such statements do not bring comfort to one who is aware that they are in the process of dying and leave that dying individual feeling unheard and alone.

The painful feelings about death and loss demand acknowledgment. They are feelings to be honored. The Death Care is a comfortable place to go, where you can share and others will listen and respect your need to be honest with your emotions about death.

At the Death Café tea and cake are usually served—a reminder that it began in the UK. There is neither agenda nor speaker, just people in small groups saying what they need to say and listening to what needs to be said, by others and perhaps to feel less afraid and not so alone.

If there is no Death Café in your area, you can start one. To learn about this organization, it history and its purpose, or to find the location of a Death Café nearest you, or if there are none in your are, how to start one, contact:
www.deathcafe.com

• • • • • • •

INTERNATIONAL ASSOCIATION FOR NEAR-DEATH STUDIES (IANDS)

In 1957, Dr. Raymond Moody's book, Life after Life was published, and millions of reader's were captivated by his stories of people who had die and came back to life and shifted how they perceived life and death. I was one of those readers. Fifty-seven years later, in a casual conversation at a group meeting, I met Barbara Bartolome, founder and director of the IANDS Chapter in Santa Barbara and member of the IANDS National Board of Directors. Interest that had lain dormant was rekindled on the spot.

In 1978, after the pioneering works of Drs. Elizabeth Kübler-Ross, Raymond Moody, and George Ritchie brought near-death experiences to the public's attention, the International Association for Near-Death Studies was founded. It is the first organization to study near-death and similar experiences and their relationship to human consciousness.

Today, its fifty chapters are located throughout the world and focus their efforts on building community for near-death experiencers, their affect on other's lives, and implications for beliefs about life and death, and human purpose. For many, working with IANDS has resolved their fear of death. To find answers to your questions about near-death experiences, or the location of a local chapter, or to start a chapter in your area, contact the IANDS website: www.iands.org

• • • • • • •

SACRED DYING

Megory Anderson's book, *Sacred Dying*, grabbed my attention and gently held it, often moving me to tears of compassion and inspiration. A new world opened. Anderson's love, common sense, and creativity teach us that often the simplest acts of caring can be the most powerful. She makes clear that one is alive until the breathing stops, and that dying is a part of living, the final act of one's life. The beauty of validating life by nurturing and tending to the dying brought comfort to me as I realized that I might bring comfort to another. It also gave me confidence and some basic skills to enable me to be there when someone is most vulnerable and needing the care and love of another. Much can be done to ease the fear and pain of entering the throes of death. With a little guidance and an abundance of compassion, Andersen shares the simplicity of showing love, of tending to life during its final time.

Often it isn't that we don't want to comfort the dying, it is that we don't have a clue about what to do when we are at the bedside of the dying. We are often afraid. Anderson's simple, genuine acts of caring inspires us, gives us confidence, and eases our fears. To those of us who want to be helpful and don't know what to do, there is now a handbook: Attending the Dying: A Handbook of Practical Guidelines. There is also an in-depth training program available online.

This book's impact is profound. Reading it shifted my feelings about being with dying, invited me to become comfortable in knowing that I could be of comfort to the dying. As I began to put the Appendix together, I Googled

Sacred Dying by Megory Anderson to see if she had written other books. There she was! Only now she is Executive Director of the Sacred Dying Foundation with a website and a program to educate and guide family members, friends, caretakers, and other professionals in being a comforting presence as they offer love and solace to the dying. Included is what she calls Vigiling. What a beautiful word! It indicates action. It tells us that there are things we can do.

Megory Anderson inspires us to be a confident, competent person who can care for someone in those final weeks, days, and hours. She shows us how to do that. Her book is inspiring. The foundation's website is informative and helpful. For information, contact:

The Sacred Dying Foundation
P.O. Box 210329
San Francisco, CA 94121
info@sacreddying.org
www.SacredDying.Org

• • • • • • • •

AGING WITH DIGNITY
AND
THE FIVE WISHES

Aging with Dignity was founded by Jim Towey and dedicated to caring for the most vulnerable among us. In 1997, working with the American Bar Association and health organizations, introduced Five Wishes, and is often referred to as, "the living will with heart and soul." It allows one to spell out one's wishes in thing that matter most: comfort, family relationships, personal dignity, and spiritual matters.

Five Wishes meets legal requirement in forty-two states, and in the remaining states can be used in conjunction with the state's required document. Five Wishes is clearly written, comes with guidance in completing the form, is free, and can be downloaded on your computer.

Empowering individuals to make decisions in advance of the time when they no longer have access to the ability to make decisions, Five Wishes also allows family members to have a clear understanding of the wishes of a loved one and guidance in carrying out those wishes. Although current sophisticated medical technology can work miracles, it often overlooks the emotional as well as spiritual aspects of illness and death and fails to include the patient's wishes as to whether or not medical treatment is appropriate. Five Wishes is clearly written, comes with guidance in completing the form, is free, and can be downloaded on your computer. For information, contact:

www.agingwithdignity.org

• • • • • • •

IT'S OK TO DIE

It is ok to die. Although the statement sounds stark, it is honest, clear, important, and courteous. Board-Certified physician, Monica Williams-Murphy, MD, and her husband, Kristian Murphy, have written a book titled,

It's OK To Die. Powerful stories of what happens when a loved one near death is rushed to ER opens our eyes to the harsh and compelling reality of making decisions during a crisis and without forethought. More often than not, the patient has not discussed what is wanted in the way of treatment; no end-of-life options have been explored; no plans have been made; no documents are in order. The grieving family, caught up in overwhelming emotional stress, must decide on the spot what medical decisions they want the attending physician to make. The prevailing emotion is "Please don't let Grandma die!" If ever a book made the case for planning ahead, this book does. We are not only convinced of the need to prepare for out deaths, there is also a thorough and well-thought-out check list that can be downloaded from their website that can lead us through the complex process of making these necessary decisions.

An inspiring, deeply moving story of one wife's courage and love holds the essence of this book. Dr. Murphy writes: Should we as a nation and culture become able to adopt the attitude taught us by Mrs. Sharply as her husband lay dying, death could again become a holy moment, woven both beautifully and sorrowfully back into the fabric of our human lives—not to shunned, avoided, denied, or ignored, but to be embraced in its power—the power of healing, love, and closure. For more information contact:

www.OKtoDie.com

• • • • • • •

HOSPICE

No list organizations offering services to the dying is complete without Hospice. This organization as we know it today was founded by Dame Cicely Saunders in 1967 in London. Today, hospice care and facilities exist throughout the world. Dedicated to the principle that life has value until one's last breath, that comfort and loving care are paramount and made possible by advances in the palliative care. For information contact:

National Hospice Foundation
1713 King Street
Alexandria, VA 22314
703-837-1500
www.nationalhospicefoundtion.org

• • • • • • • •

INFORMATION AT OUR FINGER TIPS

The miracle of the Internet offers a vast amount of information. Google:

- *End of Life Care for Elderly often too Aggressive*, by Ryan Jaslow, CBS article 2/7/13
- *The Cost of Dying*, CBS 11/22/2009 and 8/8/2010
- *Best Care: We Make It Harder Than It Has To Be* by NPR staff, 3/26/2012
- Being Prepared for the Final Days, CBS Report 4/27/2014.

Twenty years ago, Bud Hammes, PhD, medical ethicist with the Gundersen Health System, La Cross, WI started *Respecting Choices,* a program to encourage people to write down what treatment they wished during their final stage of life. Today, end-of-life directives are in place for over 90% of the population!

<u>http://www.cbsnews.com/news/being-prepared-for-the-final-days/</u>

Written preparation spelling out a detailed wishes for end-of-life care is a gift for one's family, allowing them to take the very best care of you in the way you want to be cared for. Information is everywhere.
The Internet is an essential source.

• • • • • • • •

OTHER ORGANIZATIONS

Green Burial Council:
<u>www.greenburialcouncil.org</u>

National Home Funeral Alliance:
    11014 19th Street SE
    Ste #8 PMB #155
    Everett, WA 98208
http://homefuneralalliance.org

Natural Burial Association:
<u>www.naturalburialassoc.ca</u>

• • • • • • •

RESEARCH ON AGING

The Buck Institute:
   The Buck independent research facility focuses solely on understanding the connection between aging and chronic disease. Their mission is to increase the healthy years of life Institute is the nation's first. For information:

www.buckinstitute.org

STATISTICAL INFORMATION ON AGING AND DEATH

• • • • • • • •

THE NATIONAL INSTITUTE ON AGING
www.nic.nih.gov/

• • • • • • • •

COURSES AND CLASSES

   With ever increasing interest in issues surrounding death, more educational institutions are offering courses on death-related subjects. Some universities and colleges offer courses on death and dying on a regular basis. Others offer these courses but not on a consistent basis. Check with your local community colleges and school districts that offer adult education classes to find out if courses are offered. Let the institution know the classes you are interested in taking.

• • • • • • • •

RECOMMENDED READING

Anderson, M. (2003). *Sacred Dying: Creating Rituals for Embracing the End of Life*. NY: Marlowe & Company.

Becker, E. (1993). *The Denial of Death*. NY: Free Press Paperback. A Division of Simon Shuster.

Brown, N. O. (2005). *In Memoriam: Norman O. Brown*. (J. Neu, Ed.). Santa Cruz, CA: New Pacific Press.

Byock, I. (1997). *Dying Well*. NY: Berkeley Publishing Group.

Byock, I. (2012). *The Best Possible Care: A Physician's Quest To Transform Care Through the End of Life*. NY: Penguin Group, Inc. Special Markets.

Callahan, M. & Kelly, P. (1992). *Final Gifts: Understanding the Special Awareness, Needs, and Communications of the Dying*. NY: Bantam.

Castaneda, C. (1972). *Journey to Ixtlan: The Lessons of Don Juan*. NY: Simon & Schuster.

Dalai Lama. (2002). *Advice on Dying and Living a Better Life*. NY: Arria Books.

Delbanco, N. (2011). *Lastingness: The Art of Old Age*. NY: Grand Central Publishing, Hatchet Book Group.

Hafiz. (1999). *The Gift: Poems by Hafiz, the Great Sufi Master*. (D. Ladinsky, Ed.). NY: Penguin Group.

Halifax, J. (2008). *Being with Dying: Cultivating Compassion and Fearlessness in the Presence of Death.* Boston: Shambhala.

Jacoby, S. (2011). *Never Say Die: The Myth and Marketing of the New Old Age.* NY: Pantheon.

Kearney, M. (1996). *Mortally Wounded: Stories of Soul Pain, Death, and Healing*: NY: Scribner.

Kearney, M. (2009). *Place of Healing.* New Orleans: Spring Journal.

Kiernan, S. (2006). *Last Rights: Rescuing the End of Life from the Medical System.* NY: St. Martins Press.

Krishnamurti, J. (1993). *Krishnamurti to Himself: His Last Journal.* San Francisco, CA: Harper Collins.

Krishnamurti, J. (1961). *A Walk with Krishnamurti: Daily Journ*al. San Francisco, CA: Harper Collins.

Kübler-Ross, E. (1969). *On Death and Dying.* NY: MacMillan.

Levine, S. (1997). *A Year to Live: How Best to Live this Year as if it Were Your Last.* NY: Bell Tower.

Levine, S. & Levine, O. (1989). *Who Dies? An Investigation of Conscious Living and Conscious Dying.* NY: Anchor Books: A
Division of Random House, Inc.

Nuland, S. (1995). *How we Die: Reflections on Life's Final Chapters.* NY: Vintage Books, a division of Random House, Inc.

O'Donohue, J. (1997). *Anam Cara*: *A Book of Celtic Wisdom.* NY: Harper Collins.

Villoldo, A. (2000). *Shaman, Healer, Sage.* NY: Harmony Books.

• • • • • • • •

ABOUT THE AUTHOR

Lois West Bristow, PhD, author, public speaker, and depth psychologist, began the first of her multiple careers in 1949 as a fifth-grade teacher in Redondo Beach, CA. She has taught at both elementary and junior high schools as well as community college and graduate level courses.

During the 1970s, she was owner/director of an educational consulting firm working primarily with colleges and universities but also with individual school districts and small businesses. In the 1980s, she lived in Bend, Oregon, where she was the developer of the first passive-solar townhomes built in Oregon. Later she was elected to the Deschutes County Board of Commissioners, was the second woman elected, and first to chair the board.

The Governor's economic development team named her one of seven Oregonians who made a difference.

In 1986, she received the Soroptimist International Woman of the Year recognition in Human Rights/Status of Women. She retired and relocated to her home state of California. At seventy-six, she enrolled in graduate school and five weeks after her eightieth birthday was awarded her PhD in Depth Psychology from the Pacifica Graduate Institute. The focus of her dissertation was on J.G. Jung's individuation process during the final years of life. Interspersed among careers, she has been a teacher/life coach working one-on-one to help people own their power, gain new insights, and develop their gifts in order to live more rewarding lives. Today, she writes, lectures, and maintains a small practice as a depth psychologist.

Her three children, Sheridyn, Brad, and Derek, brought her the gift of family closeness. The tragic death of her oldest son Brad brought the reality of death into focus. A mother of three, she has five grown grandchildren and one great-granddaughter.

ENDNOTES

1. Montaigne, D. Cited in Nuland, S. (1995). *How We Die: Reflections on Life's Final Chapter.* NY: Vintage Books: A Division of Random House, Inc. pp. 87-88.
2. Heidegger, M. Retrieved January 22, 2009. www.brainyquote.com/quotes/authors/m/martin_heidegger.html.
3. Byock, I. (1997). *Dying Well.* NY: Berkeley Publishing Group. p. 248.
4. Baldock, R. (1992). *Pablo Casals.* London: Victor Gollancz, LTD. p. 32.
5. Travers, P. L. (1968). *What The Bee Knows.* NY: Penguin Books. p. 29.
6. Ibid. p. 28.
7. Byock, MD. *CBS News: 60 minutes.* (Nov 23, 2009).
8. Ibid.
9. Kiernan, S. (2006). *Last Rights: Rescuing the End of Life from the Medical System.* NY: St. Martins Press. p. 44.
10. Brown, PhD, RN, T. (2010). *Critical Care: A New Nurse Faces Death, Life, and Everything in Between.* NY: HarpersStudio.
11. Ibid.
12. Kearney, M. (2008). Hospice in-service training. Santa Barbara, CA.
13. Kiernan, S. (2006). p. 44.
14. Kearney, M. (2008). Hospice in-service.
15. Kiernan, S. (2006).
16. Gupta, Sanjay, MD. (2012). *More Treatment, More Mistakes.* New York Times. July 31, 2012.
17. Nuland, S. (1995). *How We Die: Reflections on Life's Final Chapter.* NY: Vintage Books: A division of Random House, Inc. p. 43.
18. Ibid. pp. 87-88.

[19] Castaneda, C. (1972). *Journey to Ixtlan: The Lessons of Don Juan.* NY: Simon & Schuster.
[20] Grof, S. & Halifax, J. (1973). Lecture: The Center for Healing Arts. Westwood, CA.
[21] Hillman, J. (1977). *Re-visioning Psychology.* NY: HarperPerennial: Division of Harper Collins. p. x.
[22] Krishnamurti, J. (1961). *A Walk with Krishnamurti. Daily Journal.* San Francisco, CA: Harper Collins. p. 134.
[23] Jung, C. G. (1989). *Memories, Dream, Reflections.* NY: Vintage Books. p. 312.
[24] Hafiz, (1999). *The Gift: Poems by Hafiz, The Great Sufi Master.* (D. Ladinsky, Ed.). NY: Penguin Group. p. 20.
[25] Kearney, MD, M. (1977). p. 22.
[26] Ibid. p. 63.
[27] Slater, P. (1974). *Earthwalk.* NY: Doubleday. p. 2.
[28] Ibid. p. 1.
[29] Jung, C. G. (1989). Memories, Dreams, Reflections. (R. Winston & C. Winston, trans., A. Jaffé, ed.) (Revised edition.). NY: Vintage Books.
[30] Jung, C. G. (1933). *Modern Man in Search of a Soul.* (W.S. Dell & C. Baynes, Trans.) NY: Harcourt Brace. p. 193.
[31] Gibran, K. (1970). The Prophet. NY: Alfred A. Knopf.
[32] Pushkin, A. (1964). *The Poems, Prose, and Plays of Alexander Pushkin* (A. Yarmolinsky, Trans.) NY: Random House: Modern Library. p. 65.
[33] Housman, A. (1959). *Collected Poems.* NY: Henry Holt and Company. p. 232.
[34] Tennyson, A. L. (2004). *Tennyson: Poems.* London: Knoph: A division of Random House
[35] Thomas, D. (1952). *Dylan Thomas Selected Poems.* NY: New Direction Books. p. 122.
[36] Kearney, MD, M. (1997). p. 67.
[37] Kearney, MD, M. (2008). *Hospice in-service.* Santa Barbara, CA.
[38] Brown, PhD, RN, T. (2010). *Critical Care: A New Nurse Faces Death, Life, and Everything in Between.* NY: HarpersStudio.
[39] Anderson, M. (2003). *Sacred Dying: Creating Rituals for Embracing the End of Life.* NY: Marlowe & Company.
[40] Villoldo, A. (2000). *Shaman, Healer, Sage.* NY: Harmony Books. p. 4243.
[41] Ibid. p. 115.
[42] Rodriquez, S. Personal stories. Names have been changed.

[43] Buettgenbach, D. Personal stories. Names have been changed.
[44] Corbett, L. (2007). *Psyche and the Sacred*. New Orleans: Spring Journal. p. 21.
[45] Mitford, J. (1972). *The American Way of Dying*. NY: Simon & Schuster.
[46] Kübler-Ross, E. (1969). *On Death and Dying*. NY: Macmillan Publishing Company.
[47] Villoldo, A. (2005). Lecture: Scottsdale, AZ.
[48] Kearney, MD, M. (1997). pps. 62-63.
[49] Angelou, M. (1993). *Wouldn't Take Nothing for My Journey Now*. New York: Random House. p. 47.
[50] Montaigne, D. Cited in Nuland, S. (1995). p. 129.
[51] Jung, C. G. (1989). p. 275.
[52] Travers, P. L. (1968). p. 26.